Liberation South,
Liberation North

Liberation South, Liberation North

Edited by Michael Novak

Roger W. Fontaine   Sebastian Piñera

Ralph Lerner   Joseph Ramos

Sergio Molina   Juan Luis Segundo

American Enterprise Institute for Public Policy Research
Washington and London

Michael Novak is resident scholar in religion and public policy at the American Enterprise Institute and adjunct professor of religion at Syracuse University.

Library of Congress Cataloging in Publication Data

Main entry under title:
Liberation south, liberation north.

(AEI studies ; 338)
Includes bibliographical references.
Contents: Introduction / Michael Novak—Capitalism —socialism, a theological crux / Juan Luis Segundo —[etc.]
  1. Latin America—Economic conditions—1945– — Addresses, essays, lectures. 2. Latin America—Social conditions—1945–   —Addresses, essays, lectures.
3. Latin America—Politics and government—1948– —Addresses, essays, lectures. 4. Liberation theology— Addresses, essays, lectures. I. Novak, Michael.
II. Series.
HC125.L5   330.98'0038   81-17618
ISBN 0-8447-3464-0   AACR2

AEI Studies 338

Printed in the United States of America

Contents

Acknowledgments

"Capitalism—Socialism: A Theological Crux"
From *The Mystical and Political Dimension of the Christian Faith,*
Concilium vol. 96. Copyright © 1974 by Herder and Herder and
Stichting Concilium. Reprinted by permission of The Seabury Press,
New York.

"Commerce and Character: The Anglo-American as New-Model
Man"
From *The William and Mary Quarterly,* 3d Series, vol. 36, January
1979. Copyright © 1979 by the Institute of Early American History
and Culture. Reprinted by permission.

"Reflections on Gustavo Gutiérrez's Theology of Liberation"
This article was published in Spanish in *Estudios Sociales,* no. 2,
December 1973.

"Dependency and Development: An Attempt to Clarify the Issues"
This article was published in Spanish in *DOCLA,* September-October
1978.

"On the Prospects of Social Market Democracy—or Democratic
Capitalism—in Latin America"
This article was written in 1980 and appears here for the first time in
print.

"Latin America: The End of Democratic Reformism?"
This article was written in 1978 and appears here for the first time in
print.

"Extreme Poverty in Latin America"
This article was published in Spanish in *DOCLA,* September-October
1978.

"Conclusion: The Quest for Liberation"
This article was written in 1981 and appears here for the first time in
print.

Introduction

Michael Novak

America North and South has been the setting for more than one theory of liberation. Both continents were discovered by Europeans at about the same time. Both were colonized by the greatest naval powers in the world at that time, Spain and Britain. In population, the continents grew side by side—each had approximately 130 million persons in 1940—until after 1960, when the North American population leveled off at about 250 million, while that of Latin America shot up to 360 million (1980). For more than a century, South America seemed far richer than North America, yielding silver and lead to ornament the churches and public buildings of Spain, while North America produced corn, tobacco, furs, and cotton.

In 1776, in a prescient section of *An Inquiry into the Nature and Causes of the Wealth of Nations*, Adam Smith contemplated the two Americas. He urged the world to watch their quite different experiments in political economy.[1] South America chose to embody the political economy of Latin Europe, as handed down from the days of the Holy Roman Empire and adapted to American conditions. North

[1] Smith draws the comparison often. For example: "The Spanish colonies are under a government in many respects less favourable to agriculture, improvement and population, than that of the English colonies." Again: "But there are no colonies of which the progress has been more rapid than that of the English in North America. Plenty of good land, and liberty to manage their own affairs their own way, seem to be the two great causes of the prosperity of all new colonies. In the plenty of good land the English colonies of North America, though, no doubt, very abundantly provided, are, however, inferior to those of the Spaniards and Portugueze, and not superior to some of those possessed by the French before the late war. But the political institutions of the English colonies have been more favourable to the improvement and cultivation of this land, than those of any of the other three nations." Adam Smith, *An Inquiry into the Nature and Causes of the Wealth of Nations* (New York: Modern Library, 1937), pp. 203, 538–39; see especially chap. 7, p. 2, "Causes of the Prosperity of New Colonies."

1

America was more experimental and broke more thoroughly from Europe. It would try to embody *novus ordo seclorum*—a new order of the ages, a new conception of political economy.

When someone asked Benjamin Franklin if it was true that the United States had succeeded in giving birth to a republic, he replied, "Yes. If you can keep it." In 1863, at Gettysburg, Abraham Lincoln still spoke of the North American idea as an experiment, testing whether any nation so conceived could long endure. "North Americans," Professor Michael Dodson of Texas Christian University writes, "not feeling any need for self-criticism and orientation, have largely eschewed political theories and philosophies."[2] It is hard to credit such a notion when one realizes that no other nation in history has ever been so thoroughly conceived around an *idea*, a novel idea, unprecedented and improbable of success as once it seemed. North Americans were so conscious of defying all of history that, if anything, they overstressed the newness of the world they were building. They spoke often of dream, vision, covenant, compact. They were, nonetheless, an extremely practical people. The *theoria* of liberty was dear to them, even more so its *praxis*.

Trade between North America and Latin America was minimal for three centuries. Most of the industrial and technological inventions for which North America is famous appeared at the end of the nineteenth and in the twentieth centuries. The locomotive, the telegraph, the telephone, the electric light, the automobile, the airplane, television, and the computer were unknown to the seventeenth and eighteenth centuries; most did not come to be known or to be mass-produced until the twentieth century. For much of its existence, North America, like South America, depended on Europe for most of its manufactured goods.

Latin America retained the aristocratic traditions of Europe far longer than North America. Its patterns of land ownership were different; its understanding of property was dramatically different. The patterns of Latin American economic life resembled those of the southern states of the United States—the plantation system, an agrarian ethos—more than those of the northern industrial states. The economic system of South America was mercantilist or, in Max Weber's phrase, *patrinomial*; state controls and family heritage governed it; there were hardly any free markets or industry; there was not much of a middle class, little tradition of widespread home ownership, and only a little small, independent farming.[3]

[2] Michael Dodson, "Prophetic Politics and Political Theory in Latin America," *Polity*, Spring 1980, p. 389.

[3] "The mercantilist regulations of the State might develop industries, but not, or

In religion, Latin America was not merely very largely Catholic, but Latin, with greater affinity to the Catholicism of Spain, Portugal, and Italy than to the Catholicism of France, Germany, Great Britain, Ireland, and Eastern Europe. By contrast, North America had a more Protestant ethos, shared, more or less, by most of the Catholics (about one-quarter of the population) that now dwell in it. The Catholicism of Latin America was theologically more mystical, more contemplative, more traditional in tone and in temperament than that of North America. It had virtually no experience of pluralism, of the separation of church and state, of the empirical and practical temper of an industrial, scientific society. It favored the supernatural virtues—faith, hope, charity—over the natural and civic virtues. It had, in some ways, a more spiritual, less worldly tone. In other ways, Catholicism in Latin America was more intimately and integrally enmeshed in the daily texture of life, in the civic order, even in politics, than Catholicism in North America. It was closer to the soul of the culture of the people, exhibiting the qualities of a traditional folk religion in ways hardly possible for Catholicism in North America. Because of its pluralism and its status as a minority religion, North American Catholicism differed from Latin American Catholicism even more than did the Catholicism of Northern and Eastern Europe differ from that of Southern Europe.

Ironically, perhaps, the two continents of the New World have had more cultural contacts east and west, with Southern Europe and with Northern Europe respectively, than the two continents had with each other. Contacts between North America and South America have been far fewer than the contacts between either of them and Europe, in matters not only of culture, religion, language, traditions, and tourism, but also of trade, manufacturing, economics, and politics. After World War II, this pattern began to change. Exchanges at every level became far more numerous. Yet even in 1976 business corporations of North America made 65 percent of their overseas sales in Western Europe, Japan, and Canada, and only 12 percent in all of Latin America.[4] Although they are part of the same hemisphere, Latin America and North America have had surprisingly few contacts.

Certain cultural hostilities seem to lie just beneath the surface. These may be related to historical antagonisms between Spain and

---

certainly not alone, the spirit of capitalism; where they assumed a despotic, authoritarian character, they to a large extent directly hindered it." Max Weber, *The Protestant Ethic and the Spirit of Capitalism*, trans. Talcott Parsons (New York: Charles Scribner's Sons, 1958), p. 152.

[4] U.S. Bureau of the Census, *Statistical Abstract of the United States: 1979*, 100th edition (Washington, D.C., 1979), table 944.

Great Britain. A youngster educated in British traditions is not likely to study carefully the literary and other traditions of Spain; nor are youngsters of Spain likely to learn thoroughly the political and intellectual traditions of Anglo-Saxon culture. The similarity of starting place and the dissimilarity of trajectory after, say, 1850 introduced emotional elements into relations between North America and Latin America. North Americans unwittingly entertain stereotypes about Latin America, and Latin Americans about "Yanquis," which are all the stronger for the relative paucity of contacts and mutual influences.

Thus, the rationale for the present collection of essays is to advance the study of two quite different theories of liberation now current upon the two continents. For various reasons, Latin American theologians, most of whom are either European emigrants or Latin Americans who have studied in Europe (at Louvain, Tubingen, and other centers in France, Belgium, and Germany especially), do not regard North American traditions with sympathy. Their hostility is often quite tangible. It runs deeper than specifics.

For a host of reasons, the new "liberation theologians" of Latin America are sympathetic to socialism, to Marxian socialism in particular, in ways North Americans seldom have been. They seldom make an effort to understand the specific ideas and ideals of democratic capitalism. Faced with political or economic problems, they tend to think, almost spontaneously, of socialist analyses and socialist solutions. In many respects, a socialist order is closer to their own past. It is less pluralistic and more centralized, and it allows for a more intense union of church and state than does democratic pluralism of the North American type. (Clergymen in Nicaragua, for example, have served at the highest levels of the new socialist government: Miguel D'Escoto as foreign minister, Ernesto Cardinal as minister of culture and his brother, also a priest, as director of the National Literacy Program.) In a socialist system, a unitary authority governs the political system, the economic system, and the moral-cultural system. Socialism entails less of a structural break with the past than does democratic capitalism.

The essay by Juan Luis Segundo, reprinted in this study, has achieved status as a classic statement of the liberation theologians of the South. There are, however, many varieties of position and analysis among other liberation theologians. Some, for example, favor more private ownership, cooperatives, and other forms of economic independence for small farmers than Segundo appears to. Still, his essay is valuable because it defines the issue starkly.

The second essay, by Ralph Lerner of the University of Chicago, is unique because it represents a kind of North American liberation

4

theology—or philosophy, perhaps, since it is less specifically religious in tone. One may quarrel with its emphases and specific analyses, as one may quarrel with Segundo's analyses. Yet the two essays read in conjunction illustrate the enormous distances between the moral-religious presuppositions, political visions, and economic understandings of North America and Latin America.

The next four essays, by Latin specialists, approach questions of politics and economics from a nonsocialist point of view. Joseph Ramos is a Catholic and a former UN economist who is now a professor of economics at the Latin American Institute on Doctrine and Social Studies (ILADES) in Santiago, Chile, and he serves on the Regional Employment Team for Latin America and the Caribbean of the UN's International Labor Organization. He has been a consultant to the Catholic Bishops of Latin America. Sergio Molina and Sebastian Piñera have served on the UN Economic Commission for Latin America (ECLA), specializing in problems of extreme poverty. Molina was minister of finance under President Eduardo Frei of Chile. All three are nonsocialist, non-Friedmanite economists committed to democracy. Voices such as theirs are too seldom heard in debates involving the destiny of both Americas, North and Latin.

Professor Ramos's first essay evaluates a classic book by the most widely read of the Latin American socialists, Gustavo Gutiérrez. As an activist Catholic, Ramos sees much to admire in Gutiérrez. As an economist and political thinker, he raises significant questions. He pursues these questions in greater depth in subsequent essays on dependency, market democracy, and democratic reformism. Professors Molina and Piñera show that the problem of extreme poverty in Latin America is not beyond solution. It is far graver than many recognize, but it need not paralyze our minds or wills.

Roger Fontaine, former visiting scholar at the American Enterprise Institute, has added a concluding reflection on the two intellectual strains under consideration. The thinking reflected in this volume should raise the discussion of the two liberation theologies to a new level of sophistication and empirical research. When fateful decisions are being made by entire nations, between nations, and in countless individual lives and organizations, the competition of ideas is extraordinarily important. Whatever one's own commitments, it is always possible to learn more from those with whom one most disagrees than from those of like mind.

The scenario sketched by Professors Ramos, Piñera, Molina, and Fontaine seems especially hopeful. To all the authors involved, and to their original publishers, the editor is profoundly grateful.

1
Capitalism—Socialism: A Theological Crux

Juan Luis Segundo

Latin American theology, especially the theology of liberation, is re-
puted to be enthusiastic, ephemeral and rather light-weight in European theological circles, which are used to work of a more developed
character. This is naturally of some concern to us, not only because it
calls us and our work into question, but because, with rare exceptions,
Latin American seminarists continue to be academically formed by a
theology which at its best is a copy of the most reputable and up-to-
date European theology.

In the formation of the future priests and pastors in Latin
America, the theme of liberation frequently appears in a light that is
more political and kerygmatic than, properly speaking, theological.
On the other hand, it is a fact that the pastoral praxis has been especially responsible for orientating theological thought towards liberation and related themes. Hence the theology of liberation, whatever
one's view of the validity of this term, is a spoken much more than a
written theology.

It will have been repeatedly made clear in this issue of *Concilium*
that the phrase "theology of liberation" does not designate one sector
of theology (such as the "theology of work" or the "theology of
death"), but the whole of theology itself. It is theology seen not from
one of the various possible standpoints, but from the one standpoint
indicated by Christian sources as the authentic, privileged one for the
right understanding of divine revelation in Jesus Christ.[1]

Because of all these factors, I believe that the polemics about the

---

[1] Cf. Gustavo Gutiérrez, *A Theology of Liberation* (Orbis Books, Maryknoll,
N.Y., 1973) *passim*. This book, and that of Hugo Assmann, *Opresión-Liberación.
Desafío a los cristianos* (Montevideo, 1971), are as far as I know the only two
books of the theology of liberation which raise the debate to the level of a well-
documented scientific dialogue with European theology.

seriousness of the theology of liberation cannot make any advance, except through a concrete problem taken as a test. I prefer to invite the reader to accompany me in a concrete theological experience and put to theology one of the most acute human problems of my Latin American continent—the option between capitalist and socialist society.

Before beginning, I ask the reader to keep in mind one decisive datum. This option, in our case, is not made in relation to the possibilities offered by a developed capitalism or socialism. The choice we have to make is not between society as it exists in the USA or society as it exists in the Soviet Union. Our option is taken from the oppressed periphery of the great economic empires. What socio-political scheme can be chosen now from our own underdeveloped condition, which will at the same time be effective and coherent with the kind of society which we desire for Latin Americans as we know them?

This is the question we put to theology, because it is vital for us. But another question arises immediately. Is it meaningful to put such questions precisely to theology? This is not an easy question to answer.

I will not linger on the classical theological opinion, especially in Catholic circles, which would certainly be in the affirmative, though on the basis of theological assumptions which are very questionable and ultimately, to my mind, unacceptable. In the first place, the question is regarded as suitable because the option belongs to the ambit of moral theology, which has its own procedures. In the second place, it is generally added that the option for socialism is morally unacceptable, because socialism does not recognize the natural right of the human being to private ownership, even of the means of production. Neither the abysmal separation between a dogmatic theology and a moral theology, nor the notion of "natural law", nor especially its application to the defence of the private possession of such means by some people, and only some, appear to me to be principles of enough substance to merit particular attention.[2]

The two negative replies appear to me to be more subtle, profound and worthy of attention. These deny the right to put, or the suitability of putting, the capitalist-socialist option to theology. One of these negative replies is of pragmatic origin and carries more weight in Latin America, while the other is of theoretical origin and counts for more in Europe.

[2] Cf. Juan L. Segundo, *De la sociedad a la teología* (Buenos Aires, 1970), III, p. 127 ff.

I

The pragmatic negative to any consideration of our problem follows, as may be imagined, from the task which the Christian Churches attribute to themselves. As it is a pragmatic negative, it is particularly interesting for what it does not say, for its hidden reasons and motives, that is to say, for the theory which underlies it.

The refusal to decide one way or another in the problem under discussion is well exemplified in the answer given by the Catholic bishops of Chile to this vital question for that country. They said, "The Church opts for the risen Jesus. . . . The Church makes no political option—it belongs to all the people of Chile."

What is the logical assumption behind this practical reply? That it would be senseless to make an absolute value (religious, pertaining to salvation) depend on a relative value (the preference for one system —always imperfect—of political life).

In intellectual circles, the reactions against this kind of pastoral practice and its theological implications can reach the point of contempt. It is none the less true that the great majority of Christian Churches continue to be officially structured as autonomous centres of salvation. They sincerely believe in this. If they adopt progressive positions in historical matters, they do so to the absolute value of salvation which they aim to make their faithful share in even more attractive. Would it not be possible and evangelical to invert this order of values and to declare, with the gospel itself, that the sabbath is made for man and not man for the sabbath? Could this statement not be given the only possible translation, namely that human life in society, liberated as far as possible from alienations, constitutes the absolute value, and that all religious institutions, all dogmas, all the sacraments, and all the ecclesiastical authorities, have only a relative, that is, a functional value?

Once more, in Christian milieux capable of theoretical reflection, this inversion of values in accordance with the gospel is relatively easy and is operating in Latin America. But with what result? With this result—that the divergence, antipathy and separation grow deeper all the time between such Christians and the official churches which continue to be structured according to opposing principles.

To return to the point at issue, as long as the Church continues to attribute an absolute value to those objects, words, gestures and authorities which appear to form a vertical link between their faithful and God, and a purely relative value to the historical functionalism of all this, it is not possible to put to theology any question about how to orientate the option of Christians between capitalism and socialism.

We could, as I was saying, leave this question at this point and let pastoral action shoulder the task of explaining to the hierarchy of Christian Churches what the authentic scale of values must be. Perhaps then they would see the need to commit pastoral action to a human problem on the fundamental nature of the one which we are considering. But it is more and more urgent in Latin America, with this pragmatic objection still in view, to draw up as effective a theoretical criticism as possible of these mistaken pastoral motivations.

For this, we could follow the course of European theology and draw on the arsenal of tradition to show from the past how the authentic attitude of the Church towards similar problems was a distinct one in former times. We could trace the point in time when deviation set in, with increasing neglect of the functional role of the whole apparatus of the Church in relation to human history. This would be the road back to the sources, the road followed by Hans Küng, for example, in his works *Infallible?* and *The Structures of the Church.*

In my view, however, there is a very marked tendency in Latin America to approach this kind of pragmatic Church problem by another way, namely through present-day explanations founded on the psycho-social sciences.

What might be, for instance, the psycho-sociological motives for the kind of pragmatic attitudes generally found in the Church today? Latin American theology is orientated towards interdisciplinary work in this field, through the human sciences. I believe that with their help it is possible for theology to verify the following hypothesis on these same attitudes in the Church. Gestures, formulae, rites and authorities directly related to salvation, to the absolute, and so located outside the system of finalities within which everything else moves, generally give indication that those who employ them know that if they were introduced into that system they would lose not only their absolute but also their relative value. That is the danger of the absolute—either it is absolute or it is nothing. When the Churches set up as absolutes things which they are not, they seek in reality to keep a relative value for them by binding them to human insecurity. As Thorstein Veblen writes in his *Theory of the Leisure Class:*

"Only individuals of unusual temperament can in the long run keep their self-esteem when faced with the contempt of their fellow human beings. There are apparent exceptions to the rule, especially among people of strong religious convictions. But these apparent exceptions are seldom so in reality, since they rely on the supposed approval of some supernatural witness to their acts."[3]

[3] Thorstein Veblen, *Theory of the Leisure Class* (New York, 1899).

From statements like Veblen's, many scientists will no doubt tend to draw arguments against Christianity in general. Our aim on the contrary is to work across the disciplines with these sciences and *make* theology in the real sense of that phrase; this involves retracing the intimate and often unconscious mechanisms by which we think about God, his message, his Church. We believe that in the field of these inner motivating forces (which are not only theological) are found today, at the interconfessional Christian level, the profound, exciting divergences which, in other ages and with different intellectual instruments, were called Trinitarian or christological controversies.

Is it not in fact a form of heterodoxy to invert the evangelical order of values as it is now being inverted? If the interdisciplinary hypothesis is verified, it will also be verified that the heteropraxis of absolutized Churches rests on a radical heterodoxy—the progressive loss of faith in the gospel of Jesus Christ. Or, to put it another way, the loss of faith in its human functionality.[4]

The task of theology here is to classify the unsuccessful evangelical experiences which are at the base of this ecclesiastical insecurity. Another task is to establish the criteria of an authentic historical functionality of the gospel, as well as its limits, since every incarnation has limits. This leads us once more to the conviction that if the conclusion were reached that the gospel has nothing to say on a human problem so decisive as the alternative between capitalism and socialism, it is clear that it can only have an absolute, not a functional, value, that is to say, no value at all.

II

But apart from the pragmatic objection which has just been rapidly examined by way of example, I said that there is a theoretical objection to any contribution by theology to the political alternative we are examining.

What type of theology from those now practised would serve to orientate us in our choice? Doubtless the political theology or theology of revolution, which arose in the ambit of German Catholic and Protestant thought. Believe it or not, however, neither political theology nor the theology of revolution can meet our needs in the face of this most demanding political and revolutionary alternative.

As I said, Latin America wishes to plan and construct her future. Hence this critically important alternative between two systems and their respective logical arguments, both human and social. According

[4] Cf. Juan L. Segundo, *Pastoral Latinoamericana. Sus motivos ocultos* (Buenos Aires, 1972), chap. V ff.

11

to Metz, ". . . what distinguishes 'Christian eschatology' from the ideologies of the future in the East and the West, is not that it knows more, but that it knows less about that future which mankind is trying to discern, and that it persists in its lack of that knowledge."[5] Metz holds that an eschatological theology ought to know less about capitalism and socialism than the theorists of either system.

What is meant by this? That the Church is much more reticent than any political programme. Hence Metz goes on to write that the Church "must institutionalize that eschatological reserve by establishing itself as an instance of critical liberty in the face of social development in order to reject the tendency of the latter to present itself as absolute."[6]

Again we come up against the relative-absolute distinction. And again the concrete political option is considered to be relative. The difference this time is that the absolute here is not the Church but something the Church serves: the eschatological Kingdom of God, the ultimate future, which comes down from God himself to mankind.

Here the Church gives full recognition to its functionality in relation to the eschatological Kingdom. Its own triumph is not what matters to it, but the triumph of the Kingdom. So Moltmann writes: "The universalism of the crucified Christ is realized in the world only through the dialectic of taking sides. The false universalism of the Church (our first, pragmatic objection) is, on the contrary, a premature and inopportune anticipation of the Kingdom of God."[7]

According to these words of Moltmann, the functionality of the Church would consist in preventing "premature and inopportune" anticipations of the Kingdom of God. And he refers expressly to one of them: the false universalism of the Church, that is, the Church absolutized. But in the broader context of his work, it is seen that every historical project has a tendency to the same universalism, the same absolutization. Political theology attacks all kinds of absolutism, whatever their source: whether they come from the past or the future, the East or the West. It de-absolutizes on the same basis the existing order and the order projected.

For this very reason, when many of the writings of the "theology of revolution" are read, the impression is given that the revolution which is there alluded to resembles the theoretical Cartesian revolution of methodical doubt, rather than practical revolution. One may say that it revolutionizes our way of viewing politico-social systems

[5] J. B. Metz, *L'homme, Anthropocentrique chrétienne* (Paris, 1971), p. 111.
[6] *Ibid.*, p. 136.
[7] J. Moltmann, "Dieu dans la révolution," in *Discussion sur la théologie de la révolution* (Paris, 1972), p. 72.

from our establishment inside them; but it does not choose between one system and another. If it has any tendency, if it inclines to one side, it will probably be against the order established today; the capitalist order where that prevails, the socialist order where that prevails. More than that, as the two regimes coexist today, the "eschatological" criticisms converge today towards a common relativization, which is revolutionary only in name.

By another, more profoundly theological approach we reach the same conclusion, namely, that it does not do to ask theology about the relationship between the revealed message and the political option between capitalism and socialism. We have already said that this was not to be done, so as not to weigh down the absolute—the Kingdom —with the weight of the relative-transient political systems. And the profound reason is that relative values are not even fragments of the absolute value. They remain definitively within their sphere of relativity.

German political theology chooses with the utmost care the terms which indicate this relationship between a relative political order and the absolute eschatological order: anticipation (Moltmann), analogical image or analogy (Weth) and outline (Metz). All these terms systematically and expressly reject every idea of causality.

But who consecrates his life to an "analogy"? Who dies for an "outline"? Who moves a human mass, a whole people, in the name of an "anticipation"?

There is in Latin America a theological tendency which as we know has taken to calling itself the theology of liberation. Let us overlook the question as to whether the name is well chosen or what divergences may separate theologians who are included in this denomination. There is something common and basic for all of them— the view that men, on a political as well as individual basis, construct the Kingdom of God from within history now.[8] As can be seen, we cannot minimize the radical divergence which exists between this approach and the denial of causality (even an imperfect and partial causality) on principle to all political parties in relation to the definitive Kingdom.

The argument advanced by German political theology for this negation is none other than the very basis of the Reformation—the doctrine of Paul on justification by faith alone, and not by works.

One of the participants in the discussion on the theology of revolution, Rudolf Weth, outlines this argument clearly and summarizes

[8] Cf. Gustavo Gutiérrez, op. cit., p. 212 ff. Cf. also Hugo Assmann, Opresión-Liberación. Desafío a los cristianos, op. cit., p. 154 ff., and Conrado Eggers Lan, Cristianismo y nueva ideología (Buenos Aires, 1968), p. 46 ff.

it thus: "God himself effects the decisive revolutionary action for the coming of his Kingdom. That action cannot be effected or replaced by any human action."[9] Weth continues by supporting this argument with a decisive text of Luther in which the latter transfers the principle of justification by faith alone on to the plane of the universal Kingdom. Luther comments on the passage of Matthew (25. 34) in which the universal Judge calls the good to possess the Kingdom prepared for them since the beginning. He goes on, "How could [the Sons of the Kingdom] merit what already belongs to them and has been prepared for them since before they were created? It would be more exact to say that it is the Kingdom of God which merits us as possessors. . . . The Kingdom of God is already prepared. But the children of God must be prepared in view of the Kingdom, so that it is the Kingdom which merits the children, and not the children of God who merit the Kingdom."[10]

It is obvious that this exegesis radically disqualifies any option between any socio-political systems which aim to prepare in a causal manner the Kingdom of God. It will perhaps be said that this is only the sector of political theology that proceeds from the Reformation, but it is a striking fact that Roman Catholic theology in Europe, especially since Vatican II, is drawing nearer to the Lutheran positions on justification. Hence, on the points we are discussing now, no marked differences can be seen between one and the other.

If right and left are broadly identified—as occurs in Latin American usage—with the capitalist and the socialist option respectively, then we can certainly supply some proof of what has just been said. Let us take, for example, the general comment which a French Catholic theologian, Henri de Lavalette, makes about what he calls the "ambiguity" of German political theology. He writes thus: "What does it achieve? Does it divide the Church still more into right-wing Christians and left-wing Christians? Does it allow the existence in a Church with a centrist majority, of a left-wing current of thought? Or is it capable of making Christians face up to their political divisions and see them vis-à-vis reconciliation in Christ? Paul's statement that in Christ Jesus there is neither man nor woman means that the fact of being a man or woman is not an absolute which separates one from the other, allowing only one or the other to be Christians. In the same way the division between right and left—which is a political division and judgment—does not carry with it the exclusive privilege

---

[9] R. Weth, "La Théologie de la révolution dans la perspective de la justification et du royaume," in *Discussion sur la théologie de la révolution, op. cit.,* p. 86.

[10] M. Luther, *Œuvres* (Geneva, 1958), V, p. 120 (Quoted by Weth, *ibid.*).

JUAN LUIS SEGUNDO

of a Christian label, and could not be put forward as a judgment of God. The Church is open to men and women and to right and left."[11]

As can be seen from this text of Lavalette, the whole weight of theology as a serious science makes it impossible, either by way of the Church or by way of the eschatological Kingdom, for us to throw light on the practical political option which, in Latin America, is the point at which our deepest, total commitments converge.

Having reached this negative conclusion, which appears unacceptable to me, all that I can do is to say a final word about the possibilities of a theology which will be capable of making a decisive contribution to the equally decisive options of our society. In the course of this, some critical revision of the negative arguments so far presented may emerge.

III

Before studying the possible relationship between theology and the political option for capitalism or socialism, two points have to be clarified.

The first is that by "socialism" we do not mean a complete, long-term social project, endowed with a particular ideology or philosophy. We give the name of socialism to a political regime in which the ownership of the means of production is removed from individuals and handed over to higher institutions whose concern is the common good. By capitalism we understand the political regime in which the ownership of the goods of production is open to economic competition. It may be objected—why not give a more detailed account of the socialist model? Or why not speak of the possibilities of a moderate, renovated capitalism? There is one very simple reason for not doing this—we cannot foresee or control the universe of the future. The only real, possible option remaining to us is within our own countries as they are. Today the only thing we can do is to decide whether we are going to leave to individuals and private groups, or take away from them, the right to possess the means of production which exist in our countries. That is what we call the option for capitalism or socialism.

The second point that we must clarify in advance is that by theology we do not simply mean the scientific investigation of dogmas. By this is meant the study of how they came to be formulated and how, keeping in mind changes in mentality and language, they must be formulated today in order to preserve authentic continuity. As I

[11] H. de Lavalette, "Ambiguïtés de la théologie politique," in *Recherches de Sciences Religieuses*, Oct.-Dec. 1971 (Vol. 59, No. 4), p. 559.

remarked before, I believe that this scientific discipline, relatively autonomous, the concern of professionals, has for centuries now been channelling much of its content towards a conservative ideological function. This is not so much because it always proposes "conservative" dogmas, but because its very autonomy in relation to the concrete Christian praxis leaves the latter on a secondary plane, open to criteria independent of faith. So there has taken shape, in isolation from dogma, moral theology which, while it is not temporal, is profoundly similar to the civic morality required by established society. And on the other hand, the dogmatic theologian has become simply one among many purveyors of abstract culture which the consumer society accepts and even protects.

By theology we therefore understand in a much more direct fashion *fides quaerens intellectum*, faith in search of its own understanding, to orientate the historical praxis.[12] We do not accept that a single dogma can be studied under any other final criterion than that of its social impact on the praxis.[13]

Keeping in mind what we understand by socialism and what we understand by a theological task, we can consider the problem of the relationship between them. Of course there is no question of a moral theology being in any way responsible for directing the investigation. Our search is for a positive or negative relationship between dogma and socialism.

But when was dogma ever applied to political events? To begin with, it certainly was in the preaching of the great prophets of Israel. And if I am not mistaken we will see that the thought, or if you like, the theology of the prophets, has little to do with current ecclesiological assumptions or with the criteria of European political theology today.[14]

The prophet is not, of course, a seer in the modern sense of possessing ability to see into the future. But he is a seer in the sense that he discovers under the superficial event a will, a plan, an evaluation of God. But if this were all, the seer would become a legislator rather than a prophet. He is a prophet because in some way he projects into the future the historical consequences of that divine design or evaluation of events. With his vision of the divine present, he builds a project for the future which is historic and human.

An example of this kind of project was that put forward by Jeremiah when he announced to all those who were still in Jerusalem

---

[12] Cf. Gustavo Gutiérrez, *op. cit.*, all of Chap. I.
[13] Cf. H. Assmann, *op. cit.*, p. 86 ff.
[14] Cf. Gerhard von Rad, *Old Testament Theology* II (New York, 1965), *passim*.

after the exile that it was the will of Yahweh for them to remain there and not emigrate to Egypt. He associated this project so closely with God's will that he predicted to all those who emigrated to Egypt that not one of them would survive. How did the theological thinking of the prophet function? In the first place, a deeper vision than normal showed him God acting in events and judging them according to their true value. The God of Israel, being who he was (theology), could not see with other eyes what was happening. He could not attribute another value to historical facts. Starting from that conviction, the prophet imagined a future in accord with the divine evaluation, and gave it a corresponding certainty. It was a "political" project, but the prophet did not "eschatologize" it. He did not leave his hearers feeling equally critical about the historical option, which is relative, and the Kingdom of God, which is absolute.

His prophecy, considered as a vision of the future, was even disproved by events. Respecting this political fallibilty of the prophets, Henri Cazelles writes in his work on the Bible and politics: "A strange fact must be singled out in the political activity of the prophets—as a general rule it ended in political failure. But despite that failure, the disciples of the prophets collected together their oracles and recognized their validity as the word of God."[15] We can only add that as it was then, so it will always be where a prophetic theology is being exercised.

Every theology which refuses to make a theological judgment, that is, to invoke the word of God, about a political reality, on the pretext that science cannot demonstrate that the future will beyond doubt be better, draws further away from the prophetic function.

The classical prophetic stage of the Old Testament can be reproached, with some reason, for having a vision of the Kingdom of God which was not eschatological or at least very rudimentary in that respect. Eschatology is much more evident after the exile and restoration.

I, therefore, think it important to by-pass a few stages and come to the New Testament polemics between Jesus and the theology of his period, as the synoptics present it to us. I believe that very little attention has been paid to the major fact of the polemics, namely that that radical difference between one camp and the other does not lie in the theological content under debate. At least, it is due very much less to this than to a disagreement about the way to make theology and about the instruments used by one camp or the other in the theological task.

---

[15] Henri Cazelles, "Bible et politique," in *Recherches de Sciences Religieuses*, Oct.-Dec. 1971 (Vol. 59, No. 4), p. 512.

We will now consider this difference. For the moment we will put aside the current debate on the indifference or commitment of Jesus regarding politics as such. I may, however, be permitted one comment on this subject before going on. My view is that in the various attempts to show that Jesus displayed some interest in politics and in political liberation, there is an anachronistic reliance on the few data afforded by the synoptics about the relations of Jesus with the Roman Empire. For many exegetes, this constitutes the political structure of the time. To classify the political attitude of Jesus it is recalled that he had zealot (that is, seditious) disciples, that he was condemned to death as subversive of the Empire, etc.

The anachronism in all this, if I am not mistaken, consists in localizing the "political element" of the period of Jesus in the structures of the Roman Empire because they are what most resemble a modern political empire. The fact is overlooked that, at that time, the political life, the civic organization of the Jewish multitudes, their burdens, their oppression, their differing social and cultural situation, depended much less on the Roman Empire and much more on the theology ruling in the groups of scribes and pharisees. They, and not the Empire, imposed intolerable burdens on the weak and dispensed themselves from them, so establishing the true socio-political structure of Israel. To that extent, the counter-theology of Jesus was much more political than pronouncements or acts against the Roman Empire would have been.

To return, however, to the question of the confrontation of these two theologies, it should be noted that they have in common the attempt to find the divine presence and orientation in the historical events that were happening.

The theology opposed to Jesus is described in the synoptics as seeking in history for "signs from heaven" or better, "signs proceeding from heaven." With the help of the immediate context (and remembering the signs from heaven that Satan suggests to Jesus in the desert), we can characterize these signs from heaven as anticipations, outlines, analogies of a strictly divine action, something which by its very nature cannot be attributed to man or, still less, to the devil. How else can an historical happening be designated as a sign proceeding from heaven?

What are the signs opposed by Jesus to these signs from heaven? What he calls the "signs of the times": concrete transformations effected by him in the historical present, and entrusted by him to his disciples for then and for the future. It will be remembered that, to the eschatological question of the disciples of the Baptist about "he who is to come", Jesus replies with signs that are historical, relative, extremely ambiguous, at a vast distance from the absolute and definitive. The deaf hear, but what? The lame walk, but where? The sick are cured, but will they not perhaps succumb to new and more decisive illnesses? The dead rise again, but is it worth while if, after their pain and anguish, they have to yield again to death in the future? The poor receive the good news, but when will their real condition change, and who will change it?

However, here begins the different understanding of the signs, which is at the basis of the two theologies. The woman who requires signs from heaven is concerned to know whether the events, the same events which Jesus alluded to, were beyond all doubt from God, or if they could proceed from Satan. On the basis of his theology of the signs, Jesus replies with a boldness which scientific Christian theology has completely lost. He says practically the following: "The sign is in itself so clear that even if it is Satan who liberates these men from their ills, it is because the Kingdom of God has arrived and is among you." With this remark he discounts totally any theological criterion applied to history, which is not the direct and present evaluation of the event.

But it is evident that for this judgment of the event in itself, from the point of view of its human value, theology has need of an instrument of cognition which is likewise being minimized or simply neglected by scientific theology. We could call it, in modern terms, historical sensibility. In the synoptics, the decisive term constantly being employed is that of "heart": a hard, closed heart or a sensitive, open heart.

In a theological dispute concerning what was a commandment of God and what was purely human tradition, Jesus paradoxically places the commandments of God on the side of spontaneity of heart open to others, and purely human traditions on the side of reason calculating with the heart closed. In fact an event cannot be judged in itself if it does not respond to the expectation of a sensitive heart. Reason will remain paralysed before its ambiguity, and the arguments drawn from it will be no more than the servants of egoism.

It can be understood how in the evangelical polemics about the unpardonable sin, in the context of the cure of the dumb man, Jesus declares that it does not consist in theological judgment on the origin of his work—divine or satanic. Blasphemy arising from a mistaken line of argument is always pardonable. The unpardonable sin is not to recognize as liberation what truly is liberation and to use theology in order to render the liberation of a man something odious. The sin against the Spirit is not to recognize with "theological" joy a concrete liberation happening before one's eyes.

I say liberation because Luke, who is the only evangelist to describe the context of the cure, is also the only one to add a decisive trait to the parable in which Jesus describes the cosmic dimension of his work, the only theological sign that can precede the recognition of his person. With Jesus, the "strong man" who dominated and enslaved mankind is conquered and disarmed. According to Luke, the spoils of the struggle do not pass to a new master: they are distributed to their natural recipients; such as speech to the dumb man.

To end this series of characteristics of the theology of Jesus, it is important to indicate how he calls the specific instances of liberation which he effects. We have already said that the reason here comes up against ambiguous features, especially if the future is looked to. Despite this, Jesus gives these instances the most absolute name in the theology of the time: salvation. Far from de-absolutizing, we can say that he absolutizes imprudently. Just as he called cures of uncertain consequence the "arrival of the Kingdom", so he calls a momentary, ambiguous, still unrealized decision of Zacchaeus "the entry into salvation". "Your faith has saved you", he said on more than one occasion to people who obtained favours or cures (always uncertain and transient) from him.

What is the source of the invincible repugnance of modern scientific theology, especially European theology, to pronounce on political alternatives exactly parallel to the alternatives that were the object of the theology of Jesus throughout his preaching?

When the political theologian of Europe requires Latin Americans to put forward a project for a socialist society which will guarantee in advance that the evident defects of known socialist systems will be avoided, why do we not demand of Christ also that before telling a sick man who has been cured, "your faith has saved you", he should give a guarantee that that cure will not be followed by even graver illnesses.

Historical sensibility to hunger and illiteracy, for example, calls for a society where competition and profit will not be the law and where the provision of basic food and culture to an underdeveloped people will be regarded as a liberation.

In relation to future problems, this may seem of lesser importance in well-off countries. But, among us, it is plain for all to see. We live with it twenty-four hours a day. What scientific demands will prevent theology from saying, when these evils are eliminated, "your faith has saved you"? It all consists in giving theological status to an historical event in its absolute elemental simplicity: "Is it lawful on a sabbath day to do good instead of evil, to save a life instead of destroying it?"

All that has been said in the last part may seem evangelical preaching rather than a serious study of theological methodology. It is quite certain that theological methodology has long looked for its criteria in the analogy with other sciences and not in evangelical preaching. It prefers the categories and certainties of other human sciences to the apparent simplicity of the thought of Jesus, and of the primitive Church. I believe that it is necessary to translate into modern methodological terms the original demands of a theological task which will truly be an understanding of the faith confronting history.

1. The eschatological aspect of all Christian theology, far from relativizing the present, binds it to the absolute. Any effective human mobilization of resources requires this absolute relationship, but it can degenerate and this is what the eschatological element forestalls—a degeneration into inhuman rigidity or stagnation or a tendency to sacralize the existing order merely because it is there.

2. It follows that the eschatological element in Christian theology does not define its *content* vis-à-vis secular ideologies, or the function of the ecclesial community in the midst of the society around it, which is the view European political theology appears to take, either implicitly or explicitly. Eschatology affects only the *form* of theology, the way it accepts absolute commitments. The stress given to eschatological influence depends on a just evaluation, always under reassessment, of the *kairos*, that is, the liberating opportunity. The critical operation that follows from eschatology is not rectilinear but dialectic.

3. To make the Lutheran rediscovery of personal justification by faith without works the key to all biblical exegesis is quite indefensible, particularly in cosmology and ecclesiology. In other words, it is impossible to go logically from the Pauline insistence on avoiding a paralysing concern with justification of self, to the communal demands of the building of the Kingdom. The whole of Scripture is thrown off balance. What is built up in the cosmos effectively and definitively by the disinterested love of men? What does that practical violence consist of, which tears the Kingdom away from utopia and places it squarely among men? These major biblical questions have no meaning if one begins from an *a priori* position that the Kingdom is already built in all its perfection, and only awaits the entry into it of every man by faith.

4. Christian theology will have to be based much more on a sensitive appreciation of what liberates man here and now. This is opposed to the type of science which hopes to foresee and exclude now all the errors and dangers of the future by means of an adequate model, or which claims to criticize and relativize every historical step forward which cannot guarantee these safeguards. Theology has set

out to be the science of the unchangeable, in the midst of the fluctuations of human life. It must become once more, like the theology of the Gospel itself, the theology of *fidelity*, which is based on the Unchangeable, and guides the adventure of history through all the adjustments imposed by facts.

5. Consequently, theology does not find on the eschatological horizon any possibility of flying along a middle course equally above the political right and left. The right and the left are not simply two sources of social projects which are subjected to the judgment of a centrally-situated reason. As Martin Lotz observed, the objective of left-wing radicalism is the permanent opening up of society to its future. In the sixteenth edition of the Brockhaus encyclopaedia, the following definition of the left appears: "the conquest of that which is still without form, of that which is still unrealized, of that which is still in a state of utopïa."[16] For that very reason the sensibility of the left is an intrinsic feature of an authentic theology. It must be the necessary form of a reflection whose key quality is historical sensibility.

6. The relationship with a liberating event, no matter how ambiguous and provisional (as in the examples from the gospel), derives, from the strength of God himself who promotes it, a genuinely causal character with respect to the definitive Kingdom of God. This causality is partial, fragile, often erroneous and having to be remade, but it is something very different from anticipations, outlines or analogies of the Kingdom. In the face of options between racial separation and full community of rights, free international demand and supply and a balanced market (with an eye to the underprivileged countries) or capitalism and socialism, what is at stake is no mere analogy of the Kingdom. What is at stake, in a fragmentary fashion if you like, is the eschatological Kingdom itself, whose realization and revelation are awaited with anguish by the whole universe.

In my view, finally, the work of theology in Latin America is moving in the direction which I have just outlined. I am aware that a careful scrutiny of the lines of argument suggested here will lead to the conclusion that I have delivered a radical criticism of European theology, even the most progressive. I am not denying this, though

---

[16] Martin Lotz, "Le concept de révolution dans la discussion œcumenique," in *Discussion sur la théologie de libération, op. cit.*, p. 32. In the same sense, and although the word "left" is absent, the following remarks are relevant: "A solidarity of faith unites Christians with the stranger who is always unknown also . . . Christians have always had a privileged place for the prisoner, the refugee, the poor and the foreigner"; see M. de Certeau, *L'Etranger ou l'union dans la différence* (Paris, 1969), pp. 12–13. It is plain enough who (between left and right) shows continuing signs of this feeling of solidarity.

exceptions do exist. It seems to me that theology in the course of the centuries followed its own paths and, like the Church itself often enough, did not allow itself to be judged by the word of God. To get closer to that word, and to the way it becomes human thought committed to history, seems to many of us in Latin America a motive for great hope.

Translated by J. P. Donnelly

2

Commerce and Character: The Anglo-American as New-Model Man

Ralph Lerner

The hope of glory, and the ambition of princes, are not subject to arithmetical calculation.

FRANKLIN

In democracies nothing has brighter luster than commerce.

TOCQUEVILLE

Between them, Adam Smith and Alexis de Tocqueville have provided us with a detailed, fully realized portrait of the new man of commerce. Their psychological analysis—both of the universal type and of its American democratic exemplar—is by now familiar and persuasive. We no longer startle at the strange blend of limitless aspiration, quasi-heroic effort, and sensible calculation that characterizes their model man of the future. And, of course, we rarely wonder at how much domestic tranquility owes to the influence of commerce upon men's tastes, thoughts, and manners. In the eighteenth century, however, when this model of civil behavior was being formulated, all this stood in need of explication and argument. A case had to be made, and then won. The advocates—men as diverse as Montesquieu and John Adams, Adam Smith and Benjamin Franklin, David Hume and Benjamin Rush —were united at least in this: they saw in commercial republicanism a more sensible and realizable alternative to earlier notions of civic virtue and a more just alternative to the theological-political regime that had so long ruled Europe and its colonial periphery. However much these advocates differed—in their philosophic insight, in their perception of the implications of their proposal for the organization of economic life, even in the degree of their acceptance of the very com-

Mr. Lerner is a member of the Collegiate Division of the Social Sciences at the University of Chicago. He wishes to thank especially Marvin Meyers and Thomas S. Schrock for criticism and suggestions.

mercial republic they were promoting—for all this, they may be considered a band of brethren in arms.[1]

The language of campaign and contention is no empty figure, for in many respects the commercial republic is defined best by what it rejects:[2] constraints and preoccupations based on visions of perfection beyond the reach of all or most; disdain for the common, useful, and mundane; judgments founded on a man's inherited status rather than on his acts. These were characteristics of an order or orders that the advocates of the commercial republic might still (in a limited way) admire but could not recommend. They saw fit, rather, to promote a new ordering of political, economic, and social life. Further, they perceived in the Anglo-American people and setting both the matter and the fitting occasion for their great project's success.

My intention here is not to trace the philosophic reasoning that led these men to reject the foundations of the older orders. That would lead us back to Locke and Spinoza, to Hobbes and Descartes, to Bacon and Machiavelli. Consider, rather, the public speech by which eighteenth-century thinkers—European and American—sought to persuade their contemporaries to adopt maxims, conclusions, and rules of action so much at odds with the certitudes of the day before yesterday. They had first to show their audience that the old preoccupations entailed unacceptable costs and consequences. Then—a much larger task—they had to propose a new model of political and social life, sketch its leading features in some detail, develop a case for preferring

[1] In proposing to treat the advocates of commercial republicanism as a conscious collectivity I run the risk of asserting what cannot be proved for the sake of emphasizing what tends to be neglected. It was their shared commitment to ordered liberty and their desire to promote it by emancipating men from many of the modes of thought of the past that led these thinkers to commend the commercial republic in the first place. What was a republic might, in this sense, be ascertained better by regarding the sphere of liberty rather than the formal organization of a state. Thus, for Montesquieu, England was a republic masquerading as a monarchy; for Smith, the trading world as a whole was a mercantile republic. Compare Albert O. Hirschman, *The Passions and the Interests: Political Arguments for Capitalism before Its Triumph* (Princeton, N. J., 1977), esp. 100–112, for an argument that differs from the one offered here by (among other things) seeing greater significance in Smith's divergences from his predecessors and less significance in Smith's political intentions and expectations.

[2] For a recent analysis of the economic category as presupposing an emancipation from the political domain and the general run of morality, "only at the price of assuming a normative character of its own," see Louis Dumont, *From Mandeville to Marx: The Genesis and Triumph of Economic Ideology* (Chicago, 1977), esp. 26, 36, 61, 67, 106–108. A parallel treatment of this "isolation of the economic impulse" traces the Anglo-Americans' break with traditional morality but, unlike my analysis in this essay, views the result as simply amoral or morally neutral. See J. E. Crowley, *This Sheba, Self: The Conceptualization of Economic Life in Eighteenth-Century America*, Johns Hopkins University Studies in Historical and Political Science, 92d Ser., No. 2 (Baltimore, 1974), 34–49, 123–124.

it, and defend it as sufficient to cope with the shortcomings of the existing order. In all these undertakings the advocates of the commercial republic show themselves to have been uncommon men, exceptionally clear- and sharp-sighted moderns who knew what they were rejecting and why.

Prideful Pretensions Detected

The old order was preoccupied with intangible goods to an extent we now hardly ever see. The king had his glory, the nobles their honor, the Christians their salvation, the citizens of pagan antiquity their ambition to outdo others in serving the public good. However much men vied for a fine field, a good herd, a large purse, it was not by these alone that they would make their mark. So at least they said. A latter-day man might be inclined to discount these pretensions but could not dismiss them out of hand. Like Tocqueville, he might doubt "whether men were better in times of aristocracy than at other times," and he might ponder why those earlier men "talked continually about the beauties of virtue" while studying its utility "only in secret."[3] The sense of shame or pride that kept that study secret was itself a revealing social fact. To thinkers like Montesquieu, Hume, and Smith, those earlier pretensions evinced a state of mind in some respects admirable, in other respects astonishing, in most respects consequential, but at bottom absurd. A good part of the political program of these commercial republicans was getting other men to judge likewise.

Eighteenth-century men had to be brought to see how fanciful those noncommercial notions were. To the commercial republicans, aristocratic imagination and pretension were not totally devoid of social value. Honor could be specious and yet politically useful; pride could engender politesse and delicacy of taste, graces that make life easy. The weightier truth, however, was that concern with these fancies skewed public policy and public budgets, sacrificing the real needs of the people to the petty desires of their governors. As Montesquieu put it, these "imaginary needs are what the passions and foibles of those who govern ask for: the charm of an extraordinary project, the sick desire for a vain glory, and a certain impotence of mind against fantasies."[4]

It was not only the few who labored under such delusions. An entire populace might be so taken up with its peculiar vision of what

---

[3] Alexis de Tocqueville, *Democracy in America*, ed. J. P. Mayer and Max Lerner (New York, 1966), 497, hereafter cited as Tocqueville, *Democracy in America*.
[4] Montesquieu, *De l'Esprit des lois*, III, 7; IV, 2; XIII, 1.

was most important as almost to cease being recognizably human. As little as Rousseau could imagine a nation of true Christians, could Hume imagine a nation of latter-day Spartans consumed with a passion for the public good. Though the "positive and circumstantial" testimony of history kept Hume from dismissing the original Spartan regime as "a mere philosophical whim or fiction," it did not compel him to say much, if anything, good about "a people addicted to arms, who fight for honour and revenge more than pay, and are unacquainted with gain and industry, as well as pleasure."[5] If men would only recognize what is genuinely human, they would see these distorting preoccupations for the grotesques they truly were.

Disabusing the many was no small task. Those whom Smith pleased to call "the great mob of mankind" were the awe-struck admirers of wealth and greatness, of success, however well or ill deserved. Such popular presumption in favor of the powerful had its good side, too, making more bearable the obedience that the weak dared not withhold. But that was hardly the whole story, according to Smith, for men came to perceive heroic magnanimity where there was only "extravagant rashness and folly"; "the splendour of prosperity" kept them from seeing "the blackness of . . . avidity and injustice" in the acts of those in high places. Smith pointed to an escape from these conventional delusions. We have within us, he maintained, a means of distinguishing the admirable from the meretricious, the genuine from the fanciful—a means of more truly assessing both our own worth and "the real merit" of others. How, he asked, would a particular act appear to an "impartial spectator," the vicarious conscience of mankind within everyone's breast? From this uncommon vantage of common humanity, we could see what "the most successful warriors, the greatest statesmen and legislators, the eloquent founders and leaders of the most numerous and most successful sects and parties" rarely were able to see: how much of their success and splendor was owing to their excessive presumption and self-admiration. If such excess was useful and necessary—for the instigators to undertake what "a more sober mind would never have thought of," and for the rest of mankind to acquiesce and follow them—it was, nonetheless, excess bordering on insane vanity. Hardly anything Smith taught was more subversive of the older order than his cool deflation of the proud man's "self-sufficiency and absurd conceit of his own superiority."[6] He did not seek to have his readers deny or sneer at the real

---

[5] Jean-Jacques Rousseau, *Du contrat social*, IV, 8; "Of Commerce," in David Hume, *Essays Moral, Political and Literary* (Oxford, 1963), 264–266, 268–269.

[6] Adam Smith, *The Theory of Moral Sentiments* (Indianapolis, 1976), 127, 235, 405–409, 416, 420–421. See also D. D. Raphael, "The Impartial Spectator," in

differences between men but rather to discount the claims of all who presumed on those differences, real or imagined.

These presumptuous men imposed terrible costs on the whole of society—political costs that were insupportable, economic costs that were irrational. Hume believed that to some extent ambitious pretensions were self-correcting: enormous monarchies overextend themselves, condemned to repeat the chain of causes and effects that led to the ruin of Rome. In this way "human nature checks itself in its airy elevation." But another kind of preoccupation with intangible goods was less surely or easily deflected. Though Hume found no counterpart in modern times to the factional rage of ancient oligarchs and democrats, another type unknown to the pagans still persisted. It was the effect of what Hume called "parties from principle, especially abstract speculative principle." That men should divide over distinct interests was intelligible, over affection for persons and families only somewhat less so. But that they should divide, with mad and fatal consequence, in "controversy about an article of faith, which is utterly absurd and unintelligible, is not a difference in sentiment, but in a few phrases and expressions, which one party accepts of without understanding them, and the other refuses in the same manner"—that they should so divide was even more absurd than the behavior of those Moroccans who waged civil war "merely on account of their complexion." For a variety of reasons Christianity had fostered a persecuting spirit "more furious and enraged than the most cruel factions that ever arose from interest and ambition."[7] On this point Hume and the commercial republicans generally could agree with the ancients: fanaticism prompted by principle was incompatible with civility, reason, and government.

The economic costs of pursuing imaginary preoccupations might be less bloody than the political costs, but they were no less real; for proof consider the colonies in the New World. The frugal, simple, yet decent civil and ecclesiastical establishments of the English colonies were, for Smith, "an ever-memorable example at how small an expence three millions of people may not only be governed, but well governed." They also were an indictment of contrasting pretensions and practices, most notably in the Spanish and Portuguese colonies where both rich and poor suffered the oppressive consequences. A

Andrew S. Skinner and Thomas Wilson, eds., *Essays on Adam Smith* (Oxford, 1975), 86–94; Arthur O. Lovejoy, *Reflections on Human Nature* (Baltimore, 1961), 247–264; and Joseph Cropsey, *Polity and Economy: An Interpretation of the Principles of Adam Smith* (The Hague, 1957), 18–19.

[7] "Of the Balance of Power," in Hume, *Essays*, 347–348; "Of the Populousness of Ancient Nations," *ibid.*, 405; "Of Parties in General," *ibid.*, 57–61; "Of the Coalition of Parties," *ibid.*, 484–485.

plundering horde of mendicant friars "most carefully" taught the poor "that it is a duty to give, and a very great sin to refuse them their charity"; this licensed, consecrated beggary "is a most grievous tax upon the poor people." The rich, too, were ill instructed: the elaborate ceremonials in those colonies habituated the rich to vanity and expense, thereby perpetuating "the ruinous taxes of private luxury and extravagance."[8] Though vanity (as with the French) might be productive of refinement, tastefulness and luxury, as well as industry, pride (as with the Spanish) generally produced nothing but laziness, poverty, and ruin.[9] Aristocratic pride, in particular, was singled out by the commercial republicans for censure. Whatever slight sense feudal institutions might once have made, they had become atavisms, sustained by bizarre notions of honor and shame. Family pride, absorption with honor and glory, habitual indulgence of one's fancy for ornament and elegance: all these unfitted a man to perceive, let alone tend to, his "real interest." "Nothing," Smith asserted, "could be more completely absurd" than adhering to a system of entails and, by extension, to the system of thought that made entails seem sensible. Clearly, no mode of thought was less likely to render a man inclined and able to pay "an exact attention to small savings and small gains."[10] In recommending an alternative mode, the commercial republicans thought they were returning to simple reason.

Utility Resplendent

That alternative was what we today would call the market model, what Smith called "the natural system of perfect liberty and justice." This way of getting rid of a kind of unreason did not presuppose that men at large would use their reason more. Far from seconding the proud aspirations of Reason to grasp the whole of society and to

[8] Adam Smith, *An Inquiry into the Nature and Causes of the Wealth of Nations*, ed. Edwin Cannan (New York, 1937), 541, 742, hereafter cited as Smith, *Wealth of Nations*. See Cropsey, *Polity and Economy*, 33–34, on the luxury of benevolence.

[9] The distinction between these forms of excessive self-esteem is critical for Montesquieu's analysis, but the reader is left to define them for himself (*Esprit des lois*, XIX, 9–11; XX, 22). Lovejoy's attempt to impose terminological order on 18th-century discussions of the passions (*Reflections on Human Nature*, 87–117) was in the end frustrated by his many authors' "exceedingly variable and confused" usage (p. 129). Here I follow Smith in treating vanity as a man's ostentatious display undertaken in the hope that others would regard him as more splendid than he really is at the moment; and pride as the self-satisfied and severely independent behavior of a man sincerely convinced of his own superiority (*Theory of Moral Sentiments*, 410–421). See the cogent analysis of Smith's doctrine concerning pride in Cropsey, *Polity and Economy*, 49–53.

[10] Smith, *Wealth of Nations*, 362–364.

direct its complex workings in detail, the commercial republicans counseled humility. They thought human behavior was adequately accounted for by dwelling upon the wants by which men are driven —wants that are largely, though not exclusively, physical; wants that are part and parcel of the self-regarding passions; wants that cannot in most cases be satisfied. Butchers and bakers, prelates and professors —all could be understood in more or less the same way. Once the similitude of our passions was recognized (however much the objects of those passions varied from man to man), our common neediness and vulnerability became apparent. This Hobbesian truth was axiomatic for the commercial republicans. Their reason told them that a surer guide to sane behavior could be found in the operations of a nonrational mechanism, the aggregate of small, anonymous calculations of things immediately known and felt by all. It was more reasonable to rely on the impersonal concourse of buyers and sellers than on the older standard of reasoned governance for proper hints and directions precisely because the market could better reckon with the ordinary passions of ordinary men. Indeed, where the ancient polity, Christianity, and the feudal aristocracy, each in its own fashion, sought to conceal, deny, or thwart most of the common passions for private gratification and physical comfort, the commercial republic built on those passions. Seen in this light, the market, and the state that secured its preconditions, were impersonal arenas where men could sort out their wants and tend to them.[11] The openness of these institutions to attempts at satisfying all kinds of wants would especially commend them to all kinds of men.

In seeking satisfaction under the new dispensation a man needed to be at once warm and cool, impassioned and calculating, driven yet sober. Eschewing brilliance and grandeur, the new-model man of prudence followed a way of life designed to secure for himself a small but continual profit. As Smith noted, he avoided whatever "might too often interfere with the regularity of his temperance, might interrupt the steadiness of his industry, or break in upon the strictness of his frugality." He deferred present ease for greater enjoyment later; he did his duty, but beyond that minded his own business. He was, in short, a private man whose behavior "commands a certain cold esteem but seems not entitled to any very ardent love or admiration."[12] Not-

---

[11] *Ibid.*, 572, 14, 717; Smith, *Theory of Moral Sentiments*, 487–494, 417; "Of the Dignity or Meanness of Human Nature," in Hume, *Essays*, 87–88; Thomas Hobbes, *Leviathan; or the Matter, Forms and Power of a Commonwealth, Ecclesiasticall and Civil*, ed. Michael Oakeshott (Oxford, 1946), 6, 98, 138–139.

[12] Smith, *Theory of Moral Sentiments*, 350–353. See also Montesquieu, *Esprit des lois*, XX, 4.

withstanding these reservations, preoccupation with incremental gains made sense to Smith the political economist. The energies set in motion would bring forth an array of small comforts and conveniences beyond the reach or imagining of serf or savage, relieving miseries once thought fated. As men looked more to their economic interest, that interest would loom larger in their eyes and thoughts. Other concerns would matter less—sometimes because the accumulation of wealth was seen as the key to satisfying all desires, sometimes because a conflicting noneconomic interest (family feeling, attachment to a landed estate) was seen as only sentimental, illusory. It was but a short step from this awakening to the adoption of what Tocqueville called "standards of prudent and conscious mediocrity," the adjustment of production and of products to satisfy ordinary men's demands for the gratification of their wants. In the end "there is no sovereign will or national prejudice that can fight for long against cheapness."[13]

The implications of all this for how and what men think were not lost upon Montesquieu and Smith. But it remained for Tocqueville—with a commercial, if barely industrialized, Jacksonian America before him—to make the full depiction. Wherever he turned, he saw men calculating and weighing and computing. Everything had more or less utility and hence could be hefted and judged with a trader's savvy. Because knowledge was seen to be a source of power, because knowledge paid, men sought it. The market mentality shrugged off that "inconsiderate contempt for practice" typical of aristocratic ages; the *use* to which the discoveries of the mind could be put became the leading question. Tocqueville traced the modern predilection for generalizations to a "lively yet indolent" democratic ambition: generalizations yielded large returns for very small investments of thought. Among commercial republicans even religion was brought down to earth: "in the very midst of their zeal one generally sees something so quiet, so methodical, so calculated that it would seem that the head rather than the heart leads them to the foot of the altar."[14] Where the central concern was with utility, there could be little room for the play of the imagination, for poetry; men not only spoke prose but thought prose, all the days of their lives.[15]

Quiet and prosaic though such men might be, they could be passionate, energetic, and willing to run risks. Just as Montesquieu saw these qualities in England, his model commercial republic,[16] so

---

[13] Tocqueville, *Democracy in America*, 45–46, 372, 433–434, 591.

[14] *Ibid.*, 405, 424–425, 428–429, 501.

[15] *Ibid.*, 573, 585. See especially his fine contrast of the effects of slavery's presence or absence on the mores of southerners and northerners. *Ibid.*, 344–345.

[16] Montesquieu, *Esprit des lois*, XIX, 27; XX, 4.

Tocqueville saw them in America, *his* model commercial republic. Again and again he remarked on "the soaring spirit of enterprise"—a product in part of peculiarly American conditions, to be sure, but at a deeper level a natural consequence of man's freedom to indulge in "a kind of decent materialism." Restlessness goaded men on, and the prospect of happiness, like the horizon, beckoned and receded before them. Life itself became a thrilling gamble as greed and ever-changing desires elicited efforts of heroic proportions from unheroic men for unheroic objectives.[17]

No sketch of the commercial republic should neglect to stress that, as a model both for a national polity and for the entire trading world, it tended to ignore or transcend the conventional divisions within nations and among them. Its eighteenth-century proponents could realistically urge men to consider their larger interdependence without expecting (or even desiring) the neglect of national interest and identity, for commerce, properly understood and reasonably conducted, would serve both man and citizen. Commerce inclined men to consider one another primarily as demanders and suppliers, to consider the world as constituting "but a single state, of which all the [particular] societies are members."[18] Commerce was preeminently traffic in movables—things that have little if any identification with a particular state of the kind real property necessarily has. In what Adam Smith called "the great mercantile republic"—by which he meant all producers and traders of movables—the owners and employers of capital stock were properly citizens of the world and "not necessarily attached to any particular country."[19] What began as a simple recognition of our separate and common needs would end in a complex, ever-changing interdependence. Even as each labored intently to satisfy his own wants, men would become commercial cousins, cool fellow-citizens of a universal republic.

[17] Tocqueville, *Democracy in America*, 148, 225, 260–262, 319, 504–505, 633, 707. See also Marvin Meyers, *The Jacksonian Persuasion: Politics and Belief* (Stanford, Calif., 1957), 31–41.

[18] Montesquieu, *Esprit des lois*, XX, 23. See the interpretation of this attenuation of parochial passions in J. G. A. Pocock, *The Machiavellian Moment: Florentine Political Thought and the Atlantic Republican Tradition* (Princeton, N.J., 1975), 492–493.

[19] Smith, *Wealth of Nations*, 412, 800; see also 345–346, 395, 858, 880. The point is nicely illustrated by the political neutrality or indifference of late eighteenth-century Nantucket whalemen. See the editorial discussion and Jefferson's echoing of Smith's characterization of merchants in Julian P. Boyd *et al.*, eds., *The Papers of Thomas Jefferson*, XIV (Princeton, N.J., 1958), 220–221.

A More Human Alternative

This was the world—part vision, part fact—that these eighteenth-century advocates pronounced good. If others were to judge likewise, they had to understand *why* the commercial republicans preferred the market regime: they had to see that, better than any of its predecessors and alternatives, this regime suited human nature because, more than any of its predecessors and alternatives, it could be realized taking men as they are.

The contrast with and opposition to the Christian and Greek worlds could hardly have been greater. In Montesquieu's analysis it was the Christian Schoolmen—and not the commercial practices they condemned—that deserved the label criminal. In condemning something "naturally permitted or necessary," the doctrinaire and unworldly Scholastics set in train a series of misfortunes, most immediately for the Jews, more generally for Europe. Gradually, however, princes had learned to be more politic; experience taught them that toleration paid. "Happy is it for men to be in a situation in which, while their passions inspire in them the thought of being wicked, it is, nevertheless, to their interest not to be." The calculation prompted by nature or necessity overpowered the passion prompted by religion and corrected the enthusiastic excesses of those professing it.

For Montesquieu, the reliance of Greek thinkers on virtue as the support of popular government displayed an equal disregard for how men are. Political thinkers of his own time, in contrast, "speak to us only of manufacture, commerce, finance, opulence, and even of luxury." This was not a change that Montesquieu regretted.[20] According to the commercial republicans, the ancient polity rested on a distortion of almost every quality of human nature. Nowhere was this seen more clearly than in the case of Sparta. The Spartan's heroic virtue and his indifference to his own well-being were almost perfectly antithetical to the cast of the commercial republican. John Adams's characterization could serve as the verdict of all the commercial republicans: "Separated from the rest of mankind, [the Spartans] lived together, destitute of all business, pleasure, and amusement, but war and politics, pride and ambition; . . . as if fighting and intriguing, and not life and happiness, were the end of man and society. . . . Human nature perished under this frigid system of national and family pride."[21] This attack on Sparta (an extreme case if ever there was

---

[20] Montesquieu, *Esprit des lois*, XXI, 20; III, 3.

[21] Charles Francis Adams, ed., *The Works of John Adams, Second President of the United States, with a Life of the Author, Notes and Illustrations* (Boston, 1850–1856), IV, 554.

one) may be seen as a rejection of that primary reliance on virtue placed not only by the ancients but by latter-day men who drew their inspiration from classical models. Commercial republicans could reject the ancient premises even while admiring some ancient accomplishments.[22] In so doing, some may have been unaware or perplexed, and others torn between zealous wishes and sober doubts, but the foremost of them were, for these purposes, concerned less with the rare excellence of a rare individual than with what might ordinarily be expected of the generality of men.

Sparta, and the ancient world generally, accomplished astonishing feats, astonishing because they defied "the more natural and usual course of things." For Hume and his fellows, Sparta was a "prodigy," less a model than a freak. The ancient policy of preferring the greatness of the state to the happiness of the subject was "violent"; recurrence to that policy in modern times was "almost impossible." But beyond that, what sense did such a policy make? The sovereign who heeded Hume's counsel would know that "it is his best policy to comply with the common bent of mankind, and give it all the improvements of which it is susceptible. Now, according to the most natural course of things, industry, and arts, and trade, increase the power of the sovereign, as well as the happiness of the subjects." Far from being tempted to deal harshly with his subject to compel him to produce a surplus, the modern sovereign would take care to "furnish him with manufactures and commodities, [so that] he will do it of himself." This sovereign would take to heart Hume's lesson that "our passions are the only causes of labour"; he would appreciate and use the mighty engine of covetousness. And let it even be granted that the ancient policy of infusing each citizen-soldier with a passion for the public good might not be *utterly* futile, for it is at least conceivable that a community might be converted temporarily into a camp of lean and dedicated citizens. "But as these principles [of ancient citizenship] are too disinterested, and too difficult to support, it is requisite to govern men by other passions, and animate them with a spirit of avarice and industry, art and luxury."[23] With less pain—and less nobility—commercial republican principles could lead to a strong, secure polity.

---

[22] See the pithy analysis in Gerald Stourzh, *Alexander Hamilton and the Idea of Republican Government* (Stanford, Calif., 1970), 63–75; and the extensive documentation in Pocock, *Machiavellian Moment*, chaps. 14–15. Whether "the founders of Federalism were not fully aware of the extent to which their thinking involved an abandonment of the paradigm of virtue" (*ibid.*, 525) is a question that cannot be answered while dealing with aggregates.

[23] "Of Commerce," in Hume, *Essays*, 262–269.

American commercial republicans did not promote this new policy with quite the breezy equanimity of Hume. The groping, hesitation, and even anguish catalogued by Gordon Wood amply document that fact.[24] But neither did the leading Americans reject Hume's premises. In the long run, perhaps, the corruption of the republic was inevitable. Precautions might be taken to postpone that day, but the foundations were not themselves in question.[25] Again, we find in Tocqueville a distillation of what most Americans were not yet able or willing to state for themselves. The generalized expression of the commercial republican view of man and of human association was what Tocqueville called "the doctrine of self-interest properly understood," the fusing of public interest and private profit to the point where "a sort of selfishness makes [the individual] care for the state." The result was a kind of patriotism in no way to be confused with the ardent love of the ancient citizen for his city; it was less a public passion than a private conviction, a conviction arising out of private passions. Each man would come to recognize his need for involvement with others; he might even learn to temper his selfishness. Whatever else might be said of his frame of mind, there was no denying that it sustained and was sustained by commercial activity. Even as commerce reminded men of their common needs and made them more like one another and more aware of that likeness, the doctrine of self-interest properly understood taught them simply and plainly to give the dictates of "nature and necessity" their due. Human nature stood stripped of the pretensions that had kept earlier men from satisfying their natural wants.[26]

Mild Ambitions and Wild Ones

Though some might well prefer the commercial republic because it better suited men as they are, they had to look still further. Were the political ills that had beset men and nations from time out of mind less likely under the new dispensation? To what extent would the

---

[24] Gordon S. Wood, *The Creation of the American Republic, 1776–1787* (Chapel Hill, N.C., 1969).

[25] Gerald Stourzh, "Die tugendhafte Republik—Montesquieus Begriff der 'vertu' und die Anfänge der Vereinigten Staaten von Amerika," in Heinrich Fichtenau and Hermann Peichl, eds., *Österreich und Europa* (Graz, Austria, 1965), 247–267, esp. 260–262.

[26] Tocqueville, *Democracy in America*, 85, 217, 481–482, 497–499, 524–525, 602. Compare Melvin Richter's interpretation in "The Uses of Theory: Tocqueville's Adaptation of Montesquieu," in Richter, ed., *Essays in Theory and History: An Approach to the Social Sciences* (Cambridge, Mass., 1970), 95–97.

commercial republic ameliorate the self-induced miseries of political life? Its eighteenth-century proponents had high but not excessive hopes that men and nations would live in greater security as more of mankind adopted the market model. They believed that, on the whole, men would find it easier to be less cruel toward one another as they came to care more about their own safety and comfort.

Montesquieu clearly expected this to be the case in relations among the nations. "Commerce cures destructive prejudices"; it "polishes and softens barbaric morals." In making men more aware of both human variety and sameness, commerce made them less provincial and in a sense more humane. "The spirit of commerce unites nations." Driven by their mutual needs, trading partners entered into a symbiosis they could ill afford to wreck by war. They would learn how to subordinate disruptive political interests to those of commerce. Such nations, devoting themselves to a "commerce of economy," had, so to speak, a necessity to be faithful; since their object was gain, not conquest, they would be "pacific from principle."[27]

American variations on these themes were both more and less sober than the Montesquieuan original. Writing in the nonage of the American nation, Thomas Paine noted with seeming indifference that the preoccupation with commerce "diminishes the spirit both of patriotism and military defence." He could accept this diminution (once the times that tried men's souls were past) because "our plan is commerce," not "setting the world at defiance."[28] For John Jay and Alexander Hamilton, however, a reliance on the presumed pacific genius of commercial republics would be "visionary." If anything, commerce—especially when conducted in the forward American manner—would create its own occasions for aggrandizement and warfare.[29] Thus, according to Hamilton, the proposition that the *people* of a commercial republic, under the influence of the new prevailing modes of thought, had to grow less martial would not, even if true, entail a belief in an end to war. It was more likely that where the business of the people was business, the economic objections to a citizen army would be "conclusive" and war would be left to the pro-

---

[27] Montesquieu, *Esprit des lois*, XX, 1, 2, 7, 8. See Thomas L. Pangle, *Montesquieu's Philosophy of Liberalism: A Commentary on "The Spirit of the Laws"* (Chicago, 1973), 203–209. See also "Of the Jealousy of Trade," in Hume, *Essays*, 338, and the discussion by Paul E. Chamley, "The Conflict between Montesquieu and Hume," in Skinner and Wilson, eds., *Essays on Adam Smith*, 303–304.

[28] Thomas Paine, "Common Sense," in Philip S. Foner, ed., *The Life and Major Writings of Thomas Paine* (New York, 1961), 36, 20.

[29] Jacob E. Cooke, ed., *The Federalist* (Middleton, Conn., 1961), No. 4, 19–20, No. 6, 31–32, No. 11, 66, hereafter cited as *Federalist*. See Stourzh, *Hamilton and the Idea of Republican Government*, 140–150.

fessionals.[30] Generally, however, European and American commercial republicans believed that commerce gave promise of influencing international relations for the better. Like Benjamin Rush, they viewed commerce as "the means of uniting the different nations of the world together by the ties of mutual wants and obligations," as an instrument for "humanizing mankind."[31] Hamilton was the outstanding demurrer.

Even greater than these transnational benefits was the anticipated dividend in increased domestic security.[32] For Hume, the simultaneous indulgence and tempering of men's passions was almost a matter of course. Men would continue to be instructed in "the advantages of human[e] maxims above rigour and severity." Relieved of the distortions imposed by ignorance and superstition, political life would come more and more to wear a human face. "Factions are then less inveterate, revolutions less tragical, authority less severe, and seditions less frequent." Free to pursue happiness as each individual saw it, men would be able to continue to rise above their ancestors' ferocity and brutishness. Furthermore, the development of commerce and industry drew "authority and consideration to that middling rank of men, who are the best and firmest basis of public liberty."[33] Smith seconded Hume's observation, pronouncing this effect the most important of all those stemming from commerce and manufacturing. Where before men had "lived almost in a continual state of war with their neighbours, and of servile dependency upon their superiors," now they increasingly had "order and good government, and, with them, the liberty and security of individuals." The self-regarding actions of a part had led to the gradual elevation of the whole.[34]

The turmoils and revolutions of the seventeenth and eighteenth centuries demonstrated that the monopoly of public service enjoyed by the great could be broken. They also suggested how even the humblest man, by adopting and acting on commercial maxims, might serve himself and thereby the public good.[35] These lessons were not lost upon a newly emancipated order of men, whose typical member (in Smith's sketch) was an impatient "man of spirit and ambition,

[30] *Federalist*, No. 24, 156–157, No. 25, 162, No. 29, 183–184.

[31] Benjamin Rush, "Of the Mode of Education Proper in a Republic," in Dagobert D. Runes, ed., *The Selected Writings of Benjamin Rush* (New York, 1947), 94.

[32] Pangle, *Montesquieu's Philosophy of Liberalism*, 114–117, 125–130, 147–150, 197–199.

[33] "Of Refinement in the Arts," in Hume, *Essays*, 280–281, 283–284.

[34] Smith, *Wealth of Nations*, 385.

[35] Harvey C. Mansfield, Jr., "Party Government and the Settlement of 1688," *American Political Science Review*, LVIII (1964), 933–946, esp. 936, 944–945.

who is depressed by his situation." For him and his kind, escape from the mediocrity of one's station was the first order of business.[36] In principle he would stick at nothing to accomplish this. "He even looks forward with satisfaction to the prospect of foreign war or civil dissension," the attendant confusion and bloodshed creating opportunities for him to cut a figure. In the old regime such a frustrated man would have been ridiculous and might have been dangerous, but in the commercial republic he came into his own—and without having to take to the barricades. For it was above all in the world of commerce and in the polity devoted to commerce that this new man enjoyed a comparative advantage over the conventional aristocrat, over "the man of rank and distinction." The latter "shudders with horror at the thought of any situation which demands continual and long exertion of patience, industry, fortitude, and application of thought." For the new man, however, such humdrum exertions afforded the likeliest escape from detested obscurity and insignificance. His prudence consisted of a blend of foresight and self-command with a view to private advantage. His road to fame and fortune was straight and narrow; he respected the conventions of society "with an almost religious scrupulosity," of which Smith deemed him a much better example than that frequently set by "men of much more splendid talents and virtues." His virtues, indeed, were closer to the virtues of "the inferior ranks of people" than to those of the great. They were emphatically private virtues. Needless to say, they would have been altogether unfashionable in the reign of Charles II.[37]

Where such burghers were preponderant, civil life took on a distinctive coloration. The private preoccupations, the quiet virtues, the insistent passions of commercial individuals became the core of an entire system of honor. When Tocqueville looked at the Americans more than half a century later, he thought he saw a people who carried the "patient, supple, and insinuating" habits of traders into political life. He was struck by their love of order, regard for conventional morality, distrust of genius, and preference for the practical over the theoretical. He offered what he thought a sufficient explanation: "Violent political passions have little hold on men whose whole thoughts are bent on the pursuit of well-being. Their excitement about small matters makes them calm about great ones."[38] It would not be hard to regard this broad characterization of American life as at

---

[36] See Harold C. Syrett and Jacob E. Cooke, eds., *The Papers of Alexander Hamilton*, I (New York, 1961), 4.
[37] Smith, *Theory of Moral Sentiments*, 52–53, 167, 188–191, 177–178.
[38] Tocqueville, *Democracy in America*, 262–263, 612–613, 617.

best fanciful and tendentious. But any such quick dismissal probably says more about differing understandings of "great" and "small" than about the validity of Tocqueville's explanation.

Whatever else it is, this prosaic, politically cautious people was anything but sluggish. Its tastes and feelings were intense but well channeled. Thus the natural taste for comfort became an all-consuming passion, filling the imaginations and thoughts of all ranks of the people with middling expectations. "It is as hard for vices as for virtues to slip through the net of common standards." Tocqueville saw democratic ambition as "both eager and constant," but generally confined to "coveting small prizes within reach." Self-made men found it hard to shake off the prudent habits of a lifetime: "a mind cannot be gradually enlarged, like a house." Courage and heroism, too, were present, but again with a difference. Trade and navigation and colonization were with the Americans a surrogate for war. The ordeals they endured, the dangers they braved, the defeats they shrugged off were astonishing, not least because the coveted laurel was, more often than not, something comparable to being able to "sell tea a farthing cheaper than an English merchant can." From such a man of commerce, who treated all of life "like a game of chance, a time of revolution, or the day of a battle," much was to be expected and little feared.[39]

American experience confirmed Hamilton's observation that "the love of wealth [is] as domineering and enterprising a passion as that of power or glory." But it also showed that the effects of that passion could go beyond avaricious accumulation. John Adams maintained that "there is no people on earth so ambitious as the people of America." Whereas in other lands, he thought, "ambition and all its hopes are extinct," in America, where competition was free, where every office—even the highest—seemed within one's grasp, the ardor for distinction was stimulated and became general. In America "the lowest can aspire as freely as the highest." The farmer and tradesman pursued their dream of happiness as intensely as any man. Most revealing, however, were the objects of those dreams. "The post of clerk, sergeant, corporal, and even drummer and fifer, is coveted as earnestly as the best gift of major-general." No man was so humble but a passion for distinction was aroused; no object so small but it excited somebody's emulation. In Adams's Arcadian vision the general emulation taking place in a properly constituted, balanced government "makes the common people brave and enterprising" and—thanks to their ambition—"sober, industrious, and frugal. You will

[39] Ibid., 502–505, 598, 604–605, 368–370.

find among them some elegance, perhaps, but more solidity; a little pleasure, but a great deal of business."[40] The commercial republicans could, in good conscience, recommend the unleashing of men's ambition because they saw how, in the case of the Many (even including most of the traditional Few), that ambition would be tame. Political checks, powerfully supported by new social and economic aspirations, would keep men busy, wary, and safe.

What, though, of the problem posed by the others, those whom James Madison in *The Federalist* noted as "a few aspiring characters"? A philosopher or statesman concerned with promoting and sustaining a commercial republic had to be mindful of the political threat likely to arise from such individuals. What, Hamilton asked, was to be done about men whose aspirations fell only sometimes within the ordinary system of rewards held out by a republic—men of "irregular ambition," intent on seizing or even creating chances for self-promotion?[41] To this challenge the commercial republicans responded with counsel and modest hopes, but no sure solution. The limits of the market model were in sight.

John Adams's lifetime of rumination on this theme testifies to its importance—and its intractability. There was, he thought at age twenty-six, no "source of greater Evils, than the Tendency of great Parts and Genius, to imprudent sallies and a Wrong Biass." It was to "the giddy Rashness and Extravagance of the sublimest Minds" that man's bloody and tumultuous past was owed. Popular government, far from being immune, was more vulnerable to this danger than any other form. The proper course to follow was not "the general Method in Use among Persons in Power of treating such spirits." Experience indicated, rather, that "unskilfull and rough Usage" only succeeded in making genius more desperate and troublesome. Treated differently, "with a wise and delicate Management," such minds might be made into "ornaments and Blessings."[42]

Would an example of a beneficent management be Smith's proposal, in *The Wealth of Nations*, for dealing with the "ambitious and high-spirited men" of British America? Smith's premise was that free government could endure, and endure well, only if "the greater part of the leading men, the natural aristocracy of every country," had it within their power to gratify their sense of self-importance. He went on to make a suggestion that seemed to him "obvious." Present those

[40] *Federalist*, No. 6, 32; Adams, ed., *Works of John Adams*, IX, 633–634, IV, 199–200.

[41] *Federalist*, No. 57, 386, No. 59, 402, No. 72, 491–492.

[42] L. H. Butterfield *et al.*, eds., *Diary and Autobiography of John Adams*, I (Cambridge, Mass., 1961), 221–222.

colonial worthies with "a new and more dazzling object of ambition"; raise their sights from "piddling for the little prizes" offered by "the paltry raffle of colony faction" to "the great prizes which sometimes come from the wheel of the great state lottery of British politics"; direct their hopes and abilities to the imperial seat of "the great scramble."[43] Smith's was a more politic proposal than those brought forward by successive ministries and privy councils after 1763. But was it enough? A wearier and less sanguine Adams might doubt that. Among men of spirit, whose private interest could be enlisted chiefly or only through noncommercial appeals, he knew there were some few—the extreme and practically most important cases—who insisted on engrossing all the coin of pride. "This . . . is the tribe out of which proceed your patriots and heroes, and most of the great benefactors to mankind." As he confided to his old comrade, Benjamin Rush, "there is in some souls a principle of absolute levity that buoys them irresistibly into the clouds."[44] Just as prudential investments held little charm for the likes of these, so would honors shared with others not satisfy. The threat and the problem remained. In the last analysis, the only safeguard against a dangerously overreaching ambition was what Hume called the "watchful *jealousy*" of the people.[45]

Consider this modestly elevated multitude on whom the shapers of the commercial republic placed their hopes.[46] At the end, they soberly expected, ordinary farmers, mechanics, and tradesmen would

[43] Smith, *Wealth of Nations*, 586–588, 898.

[44] Adams, ed., *Works of John Adams*, VI, 248–249; John Adams to Benjamin Rush, Apr. 12, 1807, in John A. Schutz and Douglass Adair, eds., *The Spur of Fame: Dialogues of John Adams and Benjamin Rush, 1805–1813* (San Marino, Calif., 1966), 78.

[45] "Of the Liberty of the Press," in Hume, *Essays*, 10–11. This was a common theme in the period under discussion, and one on which many changes were rung. In a class apart, though, is the profound—and profoundly disquieting—discussion in Lincoln's "Young Men's Lyceum Address," Jan. 27, 1838, in Roy P. Basler *et al.*, eds., *The Collected Works of Abraham Lincoln*, I (New Brunswick, N.J., 1953), 108–115. See the interpretations by Gerald Stourzh, "Alexander Hamilton: The Theory of Empire Building" (paper delivered at the American Historical Association meeting, New York, Dec. 30, 1957); Stourzh, *Hamilton and the Idea of Republican Government*, 204–205; and Harry V. Jaffa, *Crisis of the House Divided: An Interpretation of the Issues in the Lincoln-Douglas Debates* (Garden City, N.Y., 1959), 182–232.

[46] With these commercial republicans we ought to include even Jefferson while he was extolling the chosen people of God who labor in the earth. The commercial character of agriculture in the Jeffersonian vision deserves emphasis. The rising nation spreading over a wide and fruitful land, which he contemplated, was not an agglomeration of peasants eking out a living, indifferent to the economic implications of the latest discoveries of scientific husbandry. For all his urging of household self-sufficiency, cottage industry, and the like, Jefferson thought of American agriculture clearly as a business and as a part of a world economy.

remain just that—and voters as well—busy with their own affairs, forever preoccupied with the economic side of life and without more vaulting ambition. But that did not exhaust the matter. Though the ordinary work of society remained to be done by ordinary men, the commercial republic promised these citizens literally a new birth of freedom and invested them with a new sense of self-esteem. For now, as these men collectively and for the first time assumed decisive political and social significance, they found their aspirations raised, their energies stirred and directed, their capacities enlarged.[47] They would move forward with confidence, believing that "one Man of tolerable Abilities may work great Changes, and accomplish great Affairs among Mankind" if only he brought the proper method and diligence to his task. They would move forward with no apology to those who might view their concerns as "trifling Matters not worth minding or relating," for a "seemingly low" or trivial matter, when recurring frequently, gained "Weight and Consequence." They would act on the belief that "Human Felicity is produc'd not so much by great Pieces of good Fortune that seldom happen, as by little Advantages that occur every Day."[48] Thus, in promoting their private affairs and tending to their public business—however slight or narrow —they could look forward to physical gratification, enhanced social standing, and the satisfaction of performing an acknowledged public service. Even their notions of what *is* their business grew; they would come to take a selfish interest in the public weal. This, then, was the electorate that, freed of the benighting miseries of the past, might yet be alert enough in their own interests to keep the threatening natural aristocracy in check. Given a properly contrived constitution, they might even employ that aristocracy's talents to advantage.

The commercial republicans were cautiously hopeful that the emancipation promised by their new regime would not be self-destructive. Tocqueville, taking in the scene at a later date and from a different perspective, was somewhat less hopeful. Looking beyond the jarring wishes and fears of Jacksonian America,[49] he thought he

[47] In reading the history of the life of "the youngest Son of the youngest Son for 5 Generations back" of an "obscure Family," they would learn how little ashamed he was of having no distinguished ancestry; they would have a vivid demonstration of "how little necessary all origin is to happiness, virtue, or greatness" (Leonard W. Labaree *et al.*, eds., *The Autobiography of Benjamin Franklin* [New Haven, Conn., 1964], 46, 50, 137). In the details of this individual's career they might easily glimpse their own career, "the manners and situation of *a rising* people" (*ibid.*, 135). The last two quotations are from a letter by Benjamin Vaughan, Jan. 31, 1783, which Franklin intended to insert in his autobiography.

[48] *Ibid.*, 163, 207.

[49] Meyers, *Jacksonian Persuasion*, 4–23, 92–107.

saw how a preoccupied electorate might turn into an indifferent crowd, how a "people passionately bent on physical pleasures" might come to regard the exercise of their political rights as "a tiresome inconvenience," a trivial distraction from "the serious business of life." He thought he saw how, with their anxieties fueled by a self-contradictory hedonism, such a people might readily hand over their liberties to whatever able and ambitious man promised them the untroubled enjoyment of their private pursuits.[50] Alternatively, they might slide —quietly, mindlessly—into a bondage altogether new, where "not a person, or a class . . . , but society itself holds the end of the chain." Either way they would lose their liberty and their very character as men and citizens.[51] It was in anticipation of this Tocquevillean nightmare that Rousseau inveighed against those who would rather hire a representative than spare the time to govern themselves, and rather pay taxes than serve the community with their bodies. Absorbed in their ledgers and accounts, they stood to lose all. "The word 'finance,' " Rousseau wrote, "is slave language; it has no place in the city's lexicon."[52]

Assessing Benefits and Costs

Although the founding fathers of commercial republicanism were neither money-grubbers nor philistines nor indifferent citizens, Rousseau's statement could not be farther from their conclusion. In the last analysis, commerce commended itself to them because it promised a cure for destructive prejudices and irrational enthusiasms, many of them clerically inspired. Commerce was an engine that would assault and level the remaining outposts of pride in all its forms: family pride, aristocratic pride, pride that concealed from "mankind that they were children of the same father, and members of one great family," pride in "learning" (which Rush distinguished sharply from "useful knowledge"), pride in whatever led men to believe that they could rise above the workaday world. Commerce, like the plain teachings of the Gospels, like useful knowledge, would humble the mind, soften the heart, help bring "the ancient citizen to a level with the men of [only] yesterday," and assimilate all men everywhere to one another.[53] If, in a sense, commerce imposed a ceiling upon some

[50] Tocqueville, *Democracy in America*, 503, 508–509, 511–512, 613.

[51] *Ibid.*, 667–668; and see 641–680, *passim*.

[52] Rousseau, *Contrat social*, III, 15.

[53] Rush, "Of the Mode of Education," in Runes, ed., *Selected Writings of Rush*, 94; "Observations upon the Study of the Latin and Greek Languages," in Benjamin Rush, *Essays, Literary, Moral and Philosophical*, 2d ed. (Philadelphia, 1806), 43; "Leonidas" [Benjamin Rush], "The Subject of an American Navy," *Pennsylvania Gazette*, July 31, 1782.

men's aspirations, it more significantly also supplied most men with a floor to stand on. Commercial men would come at last to regard themselves and their societies as members of a single universal state, a brotherhood of demanders and suppliers.

That this triumph of commerce would entail significant human losses was a foregone conclusion for these commercial republicans. Nonetheless, they were prepared to accept those losses, even as they sought ways to mitigate them. For Montesquieu, a regime dedicated to commerce partook less of a union of fellow citizens, bound together by ties of friendship, than of an alliance of contracting parties, intent on maximizing their freedom of choice through a confederation of convenience. It was in this character of an alliance that men found themselves cut off from one another or, rather, linked to one another principally through a market mechanism. It was a world in which everything had its price—and, accordingly, its sellers and buyers. Not surprisingly, the habits of close calculation and "exact justice" appropriate to one kind of activity were extended to all kinds, and political community was replaced by a marketplace of arm's-length transactions.[54]

Smith was even more explicit and detailed than Montesquieu in assessing "the disadvantages of a commercial spirit." He saw it as bringing about a narrowing and demeaning of men's souls, with the "heroic spirit" being "almost entirely extinguished." As in his discussion of the effects of the division of labor upon "the great body of the people," Smith squarely faced the debasement implicit in his scheme of civilization. Whether his proposals for public education would forfend the predicted "mental mutilation," "gross ignorance and stupidity," and corruption of "all the nobler parts of the human character," is not my present question. I note here only that Smith recognized the need that civilized society had for civilized men, a kind that his society normally would not nurture.[55]

The American commercial republicans who struggled with this problem sought a solution in some passion or pride that might vie with the love of wealth. For them, America's dedication to commerce was both fitting and frightening. On the one hand, it would take commerce and all the energies it could command to exploit the

[54] Montesquieu, *Esprit des lois*, XIX, 27; XX, 2; Aristotle, *Politics*, III, 9, 1280^b, 6–11. See also Richard Jackson to Benjamin Franklin, June 17, 1755, in Leonard W. Labaree *et al.*, eds., *The Papers of Benjamin Franklin*, VI (New Haven, Conn., 1963), 81.

[55] Edwin Cannan, ed., *Lectures on Justice, Police, Revenue and Arms, Delivered at the University of Glasgow by Adam Smith, Reported by a Student in 1763* (Oxford, 1896), 259; Smith, *Wealth of Nations*, 734–740, 744–748. See Cropsey, *Polity and Economy*, 88–95.

opportunities offered by the new land.[56] Modern statesmen, such as Hamilton, were mindful of how effectively commerce moved men. "By multiplying the means of gratification, by promoting the introduction and circulation of the precious metals, those darling objects of human avarice and enterprise, it [that is, commercial prosperity] serves to vivify and invigorate the channels of industry, and to make them flow with greater activity and copiousness. The assiduous merchant, the laborious husbandman, the active mechanic, and the industrious manufacturer, all orders of men look forward with eager expectation and growing alacrity to this pleasing reward of their toils."[57] Discerning statesmen, such as Adams, also understood how, in certain European lands, it was in the general interest for the nobility to affect "that kind of pride, which looks down on commerce and manufactures as degrading." Reinforced by "the pompous trumpery of ensigns, armorials, and escutcheons," "the proud frivolities of heraldry," aristocratic prejudice might retard "the whole nation from being entirely delivered up to the spirit of avarice." Though these particular pretensions could only be considered mischievous and ridiculous in America,[58] the need for some countermeasures persisted. For in this respect America was no exception: an unrestrained indulgence in the passion for wealth would lead only to "cowardice, and a selfish, unsocial meanness," "a sordid scramble for money." To save "our bedollared country" from "the universal gangrene of avarice," Adams suggested making republican use of the rivals of ambition and pride of birth, thereby employing "one prejudice to counteract another."[59] All this befitted a man who knew something of himself and had hopes for his son. Individuals and indeed families might reasonably cherish qualities that set them apart and above—for example, a deserved reputation for public service in

[56] "We occupy a new country. Our principal business should be to explore and apply its resources, all of which press us to enterprise and haste. Under these circumstances, to spend four or five years in learning two dead languages, is to turn our backs upon a gold mine, in order to amuse ourselves in catching butterflies" ("Observations upon the Study of the Latin and Greek Languages," in Rush, *Essays*, 39).

[57] *Federalist*, No. 12, 73–74.

[58] Adams, ed., *Works of John Adams*, IV, 395. See also John Adams to James Warren, July 4, 1786, in Worthington C. Ford, ed., *Warren-Adams Letters: Being Chiefly a Correspondence among John Adams, Samuel Adams, and James Warren*, II (Massachusetts Historical Society, *Collections*, LXXIII [Boston, 1925]), 277.

[59] Adams, ed., *Works of John Adams*, VI, 270–271; Adams to Rush, June 20, 1808, in Schutz and Adair, eds., *Spur of Fame*, 110–111. See Mercy Warren, *History of the Rise, Progress and Termination of the American Revolution, Interspersed with Biographical, Political and Moral Observations*, III (Boston, 1804), 415.

war and peace.[60] In a commercial republic such pretensions would be manageable, even indispensable. The solution, however, remained an uneasy one, and Adams himself wavered between hope and despair for his country.

Benjamin Rush's ambivalence toward commercialism is especially revealing. Though he did not think commercial wealth was necessarily fatal to republican liberty, he hastened to add parenthetically, "provided that commerce is not in the souls of men." For commerce, "when pursued closely, sinks the man into a machine."[61] And yet when considering the mode of education proper in a republic, he exalted commerce as right for America and for mankind. However much his taste as a private man was offended by a merchant class who "have little relish for the 'feast of reason and the flow of soul,'"[62] as a public man Rush could only be pleased by the promotion and triumph of the commercial mode of thought. "I consider commerce in a much higher light [than as a means of promoting public prosperity] when I recommend the study of it in republican seminaries. I view it as the best security against the influence of hereditary monopolies of land, and therefore, the surest protection against aristocracy."[63] In this perspective, the costs of commerce could be borne gladly.

The American Terminus

In the beginning, Locke asserted, all the world was America. In the end, Tocqueville predicted, all the world would be American. To speak of America, then, was to speak of man's fate, perhaps even of a divine decree. This country's rapid passage from a Lockean state of nature to a Tocquevillean democracy instructively telescoped the creation or emergence of the new man of commerce. The American democrat was the man of the future, an exemplar for humanity. He had adopted habits of mind and action that could not fail to be intelligible and attractive to most men everywhere. So, at any rate, Tocqueville thought; and in this he was not alone. In setting forth the American commercial republican as the new-model man, Tocqueville was simultaneously predicting and prescribing. In each case,

[60] Peter Shaw, *The Character of John Adams* (Chapel Hill, N.C., 1976), 198–199, 232–235, 241, 315–316.
[61] L. H. Butterfield, ed., *Letters of Benjamin Rush*, I (Princeton, N.J., 1951), 285, 85. See also Crowley, *This Sheba, Self,* 99, 152.
[62] Butterfield, ed., *Letters of Rush*, I, 85. Rush was quoting from Pope's *Imitations of Horace: Satires,* Bk. 2, sat. 1, line 127.
[63] Rush, "Of the Mode of Education," in Runes, ed., *Selected Writings of Rush,* 94.

however, he was beset by foreseeable certainties and by a sense that "the spirit of man walks through the night."[64] If we draw back from the margin of the providentially predestined circle and confine our speculations to things we can see with our own eyes, the reasons for his prescription emerge clearly enough.

Consider the spectacle of a united people spreading relentlessly over the land, a people who for all their present or future diversities and divisions were made one and kept one by their social state and by their habits, manners, and opinions. Whatever the future might bring, "the great Anglo-American family" would remain kinsmen by virtue of their equality of social condition, their taste for physical well-being, and their single-minded enterprise in seeking to gratify that taste. That much, at least, would remain both common and constant; "all else is doubtful, but that is sure."[65] Lifting our gaze above the fortuitous and peculiarly American features of this scene, we can detect what Tocqueville deemed fundamental for all men and all places in the new world aborning. As "the great bond of humanity is drawn tighter," men would become more equal, more comfortable, and more alike in conforming to some middling standard. Much of what set people against people and country against country would loosen its grip; all men, in a sense, would become votaries at the same shrine.[66] To this extent, the realm of freedom would be constricted. But though we are fated to live our lives as members of the new egalitarian cosmopolitan regime, we are not without choices, choices that tax to the limit our strength, our will, and our art.[67] The province of statesmanship or of political science is preserved with Tocqueville's assurance (at the end of the second volume of *Democracy in America*) that it is up to us "whether equality is to lead to servitude or freedom, knowledge or barbarism, prosperity or wretchedness."[68] It is in the light of *that* choice that Tocqueville's recommendations are to be understood: a recommendation of the commercial republic, and a recommendation of those means consistent with the regime that are most likely to foster freedom, knowledge, and prosperity.

There was much in the commercial republic that Tocqueville found distasteful: its discreet sensualism, the counting-house character of its politics, the stifling of public spirit by the petty concerns of

---

[64] Tocqueville, *Democracy in America*, 677.
[65] *Ibid.*, 376–378.
[66] *Ibid.*, 678–679.
[67] *Ibid.*, 679–680, 649, and cf. 55.
[68] *Ibid.*, 680.

private life. But beyond the commercial republic, beyond "America," was the alternative: not Greece or Rome, not "China,"[69] but "Russia." The grand and awesome alternatives with which Tocqueville ended *Democracy in America* were prefigured (at the conclusion of the first volume) by the contrast between "Russia" and "America." He insisted that the servitude and centralization of the one were as compatible with egalitarianism as were the freedom and individualism of the other.[70] Indeed, that equality of condition which Tocqueville would have us regard as a providential fact, a fated certainty, might more easily be manifest in servitude than in the kind of independence that crumbles into anarchy.[71] If, in one sense, "Russia" is literally Russia —a harsh, barbarous despotism, an atavism totally apart from the modern egalitarian tendency—in another sense it may be Tocqueville's relevant cautionary example of the vast and terrible power that can be generated by uniformity and concentration. The saving grace of "America," then, and of the commercial republic for which it stands, is the way in which it "relies on personal interest and gives free scope to the unguided strength and common sense of individuals."[72] "Trade makes men independent of one another and gives them a high idea of their personal importance; it leads them to want to manage their own affairs and teaches them how to succeed therein."[73] But for all its utility, even necessity, commerce may not be sufficient. For though commerce was part of Tocqueville's solution, it also was part of Tocqueville's problem. To counter the forces that press in on modern men and narrow their souls, Tocqueville looked to the commercial man's predisposition to liberty. Yet commerce may also predispose men to acquiesce in a new type of oppression—not the naked personal power of a Muscovite czar, but the gloved and masked impersonal power of a modern "sovereign, whatever its origin or constitution or name." Faced with an alternative that would degrade men into "a flock of timid and hard-working animals,"[74] Tocqueville searched for the highest grounds on which he could justify men's "strongest remaining guarantee against themselves."[75]

---

[69] A code-word for the limp, prosperous barbarism that a civilized people can impose on itself. *Ibid.*, 82, n. 50, 431, 512, 605–606.

[70] Consider an analogous kind of equality of condition that Tocqueville saw as having prevailed in the Roman empire at the time of Christianity's origin. *Ibid.*, 411.

[71] *Ibid.*, 643.

[72] *Ibid.*, 378–379.

[73] *Ibid.*, 612.

[74] *Ibid.*, 666–668, 675.

[75] *Ibid.*, 499.

That search led him to "the doctrine of self-interest as preached in America." Most generally stated, men are more preoccupied with wants they feel than with needs they must reason about. And oddly enough, a system that frees men to try to satisfy their physical wants is more apt than any likely alternative to lead them to see their need for liberty. More apt, that is, if their egoism were enlightened, if each (as with the Americans) "has the sense to sacrifice some of his private interests to save the rest." But where a political system failed to instruct and encourage men in this calculated self-restraint and failed to show them that what is right may also be useful, there could be neither freedom nor public peace nor social stability. Where each (as with the Europeans) insisted on keeping the lot for himself, he often ended up losing the lot.[76] Tocqueville, like some predecessors of his, could praise and recommend the commercial republican way of life because it can go beyond accommodating itself to our weaknesses. It also invites us to "try to attain that form of greatness and of happiness which is proper to ourselves."[77] Tocqueville, like a successor of his, might well have called this the last, best hope of earth.

[76] *Ibid.*
[77] *Ibid.*, 679.

3

Reflections on Gustavo Gutiérrez's Theology of Liberation

Joseph Ramos

Christians in Latin America have been startled in the last few years by an increasing number of declarations, movements, and even guerrilla actions by some of their best clergy in favor of national "liberation" and socialism. Nevertheless, however dedicated, these have been a minority, and a minority more prone to action than to theoretical elaboration. Consequently, their impact could be minimized, by pointing out the theoretical deficiencies of their actions or by attributing their new commitment to a specific individual calling. As a result, up to now, the Church, the vast majority of both her hierarchy and laity, has been able to avoid taking a favorable stance toward these socialisms, in the wholehearted and unmistakable way that these "new Christians" do. Herein lies the vital importance of Gustavo Gutiérrez's book. For it is a theological argument written not to justify isolated cases of individuals who fight for socialism as a way to fulfill their Christian calling, but to induce, if not to force, the Church, her hierarchy as well as the laity, to take a stand, here and now, in favor of socialism and against current underdevelopment, or risk betraying her Christian vocation.

How does Father Gutiérrez reach this conclusion? He starts from an experience, basic to many Christians in our continent: organized Christianity seems to have little to say about the main problem of our era—the prevailing underdevelopment and injustice in Latin America. To him it is impossible, as it is to many others—including, I might add, myself—to live his Christianity, the fundamental reason of life itself, without relating it to the main social task of our time: achieving development.

This article is a discussion of Gustavo Gutiérrez, *Theology of Liberation* (Lima, Peru: Perspectivas. Editorial Universitaria, CEP, 1971).

"Theology of Liberation" and Theology

Gutiérrez considers Catholicism to suffer from a series of internal restraints that inhibit effective action in favor of the oppressed. Among these restraints he cites the preoccupation with individual sin, and the corresponding neglect of social or structural sin. This latter, to be sure, is also the work of individuals but of individuals acting through social structures. This exaggerated emphasis on personal sin is essentially due to our individualistic concept of salvation. For it is, in the last analysis, individuals and not groups who are saved or condemned. In view of this, Gutiérrez concludes that it is necessary to reformulate the question of the relation between liberation (or the civilizing mission) and salvation, if we are ever going to be able to overcome these inhibitions and take an effective position in favor of the oppressed.

A clearer understanding of the relationship between liberation and salvation and the issues involved can be had, if we first try to analyze the less complex problem of human slavery rather than the present problem of underdevelopment. Can a slave, a person deprived of his liberty, save himself (or be condemned)? Theologians have generally agreed that he can, because each person will be judged according to his possibilities of action, whether they be few or many. Restrained and coerced though he be, the slave still preserves a sphere of action of his own. No one can limit his internal liberty. But there is more. Not only does slavery not render salvation impossible, but it simply does not affect it at all! For, in the end, we will not be judged according to our worldly achievements, but rather for the way in which we used the means, however limited, at our disposal. In this way all theological schools conclude that not even slavery, the maximum expression of oppression and human underdevelopment, will in any way deter our possibility of salvation. If this is true of slavery, so too must it be true that no other form of oppression can impede the individual's ultimate destiny (salvation).

It is not difficult to understand, therefore, why a strong current of theological opinion, I dare say the strongest up to the present, the so-called eschatological or ascetic school, tends to scorn historical progress, the civilizing mission, the development of human capacities, by countering that in the ultimate analysis such considerations do not in the least affect the salvation of man, either positively or negatively. Though the development of the person may be promoted and enhanced by other persons or by the community at large or by adequate social structures, in the end, this liberation of man contributes nothing to his personal salvation. For salvation is necessarily and exclusively the voluntary and personal work of each individual before God.

Yet there is another theological school of thought (incarnational or humanist) which also acknowledges that the condition of slavery has no bearing on the ultimate salvation of the slave, but all the same calls attention to the injustice involved in slavery, that is to say, that the development of some persons is gained at the expense of the labor and will of others. In the same way that robbery does not cease to be an unjust action because it merely deprives the owner of his worldly goods without affecting his salvation, neither does the imposition of slavery cease to be unjust because it does not affect the salvation of those whose "worldly" freedom it deprives. Thus emancipation, even though it in no way aids their salvation, is a just action, because it gives back to the slaves what is rightfully theirs. The abolition of slavery then promotes human development (a good) although by itself it does not bring any closer salvation (the supreme good). Nevertheless, since, in the end, one cannot aid the salvation of another because this depends exclusively on the free decision of the affected party, furthering human development constitutes the greatest good one person can do for another. And such human development can be promoted, note well, against or independent of the will of the other.

With this, one of the fundamental and apparently boldest theses of Gutiérrez is demonstrated: the salvation of man involves worldly liberation. But take note. This does not mean that the salvation of the *other* (the slave, for example) requires his previous liberation. Rather, *it implies that our own salvation requires us to struggle for the worldly liberation of the other* (the slave in this case). Although the liberation of the other will never be sufficient for *his* salvation, this action of ours in his favor can be the path to *our* own salvation as it is the most effective way to love our neighbor. Although our love for our neighbor sets him in the path towards his own salvation, the most it can promise him is some progress in human development, if it is not accompanied by the full participation of the affected party. The most one can do is to give his life for the other (sacrifice his own human development for that of the other), but not even our love, indeed not even the love of Christ, can assure the salvation of the other.

In this light, the mission of civilizing the world proves critical for development; so, to struggle for liberation is to struggle for building the Kingdom of God. Yet this does not imply that the struggle for the Kingdom of God is the simple equivalent of the historical struggle for progress. Although each step towards the liberation of man from social injustice is a redeeming act (for the actor) and at the same time is liberating (for the receiver), the growth of the Kingdom does not end with social liberation. "Not only is the growth of the Kingdom not reduced to mere historical progress, but indeed it is thanks to the Word received in faith, that *the fundamental obstacle to the Kingdom, sin, is revealed to us as the root of all suffering and injustice;* and the meaning of the Kingdom's growth is revealed to us as the ultimate condition for a just society and a new man."

Gutiérrez's position is thus not an easy Rousseauian utopianism. In this, his thought is rooted in the oldest Christian traditions. Sin is not merely a product or reflection of unjust social structures but rather is a consequence of that intrinsic ambivalence yet to be resolved within each man in his most intimate self. This ambivalence in man makes any structure susceptible to corruption, even when some structures (for example, slavery) are in themselves unjust.

No structure can assure human liberation even in the temporal realm so long as sin is not overcome, for liberation from sin is the only definitive liberation. Consequently, human history will always be an open process, not fully determined, because sin and personal liberty are a part of the "infrastructure." Overcoming sin is a personal action of the subject quite unrelated to his structural conditioning.

Is it not strange, nonetheless, that God asks us to help our neighbor in an area which is strictly secondary (his worldly development) and hinders us, by the very nature of human liberty, from helping him obtain something which is really vital, his salvation? Incarnational theologians answer that the existence of human potentialities is a call for their fulfillment. As is suggested by the parable of the talents: our call to God is a call to love Him with all our being, by all the social or individual means within the reach of creation. Although it is true that human development (the civilizing work) does not guarantee salvation, it enlarges our capacity to love (or reject) God. The civilizing mission is thus a condition for God to be fully glorified by all His creation. It is not only a path for our own salvation, but it enlarges the capacity of others (although it does not assure it) to glorify God. Thus our love of neighbor—though incapable of affecting our neighbor's final destiny—affects ours, at the same time as it promotes his human development.

Now, the most effective way to work for human progress today —and not only in our era, although especially in the present—may well consist in changing the structures that impede development and not just in improving interpersonal relations within these structures. For example, really and effectively to love our neighbor does not consist in bettering relations between masters and slaves but in abolishing slavery as an institution (aware, of course, that this is not the only unjust structure that must be overcome). Our love towards our neighbor, therefore, is measured not only in terms of our treatment of others but also in our efforts to change unjust structures.

The conclusion of Gutiérrez's theological reflection is that the civilizing mission, which at present in Latin America is the struggle against underdevelopment and the poverty of the large majority, is the main way of fulfilling the Christian vocation today. It was not always this way, for heretofore, in the past, the means did not exist for overcoming underdevelopment. The urgency to overcome this problem in our era is not due to the low living standards of the vast majority—for this has always been so—but rather stems from the fact that for the first time in history it is no longer necessary for them to live in poverty. It is now possible that the majority attain a decent living standard, because, thanks to technology, nature is no longer the limiting factor it once was. Today the obstacles to development are human. They are the product of unjust and deficient social organizations.

I find Gutiérrez's theological reasoning quite convincing. My discrepancies, perhaps a reflection of my professional discipline as an economist, emerge not from his theological position, but from his position regarding the social doctrine of the Church and the social sciences, and more concretely his socialist route to liberation.

"Theology of Liberation" and the Social Sciences

Although some may disagree as to the exact importance of the struggle against poverty and injustice, few are against the liberation of the oppressed. The problem consists in indicating the specific forms of oppression and injustice and in diagnosing their causes. For simply denouncing oppression in general, as is done in the typical ecclesiastical pronouncement, carries little force and is of limited effectiveness.

Gutiérrez is very aware of this problem. Consequently he devotes a number of chapters to a "scientific" analysis of the causes of underdevelopment. In so doing, Gutiérrez adopts a very respectable position, well known in vanguard circles today.

"The underdevelopment of poor nations, as a global social fact, is then unmasked as the historical sub-product of the development of other countries. In fact, the dynamics of the capitalist system leads to the establishment of a center and a periphery, simultaneously generating progress and riches for the few, and social disequilibrium, political tensions and poverty for the majority."

The state of poverty of the majorities in Latin America is hence due to its capitalist and dependent structures. Its resolution requires an independent, noncapitalist road, or, in Gutiérrez's own terms, liberation requires socialist structures. The liberation from private property is the decisive liberation in this stage of human development, because it constitutes the fundamental structural bottle-neck (even though it is not the last or most fundamental).[1]

By so arguing, Gutiérrez's attack on poverty is effective or, at least, concrete because he purports to explain its fundamental causes as well as indicate its solution. However, in my estimation, what he presents as the product of scientific analysis is at the most *one* possible explanation among many, which includes as many problems as it presumes to solve. Among these are:

1. The exploitation of one people by another has existed since the beginning of history. However, until the Industrial Revolution, no people, no matter how exploitative or imperialistic they were, could reach a generalized, sustained level of economic development. Might it not be, then, that the development of the center was due to its systematic exploitation of nature through technology (an unknown phenomenon before the Industrial Revolution), rather than to its colonization of the periphery? The cases of England and Spain are very illuminating in this respect.

Might it not be that the ease with which Gutiérrez supposes that the development of the center takes place at the expense of the underdevelopment of the periphery, is due to his supposition that economic relations are essentially and exclusively conflictive, as if the economy were static, implying that the gains of some are necessarily equal to the losses of others? We will take a closer look at the ideological preconceptions of this position and what they imply further on.

2. Although it is very attractive to place the fundamental blame for our problems on dependency (and by so doing blame others), might not this dependence rather be a reflection of the internal obstacles to development which are encountered within our countries? After all, each presently developed country has had to overcome this state of dependency. How can we explain the fact that some countries have been able to overcome it? The United States broke out of its dependency on what was then the greatest world power, while Latin

---

[1] He argues that there will be other liberations further on till we arrive at a point where sin is overcome, which will permit not only real human brotherhood and the establishment of a just society where people come together for the common good, but also the development of the new man, the coming of the Kingdom and communion with God.

America, colonized at the same time, still fails to do so. Moreover, is it not possible that, even without dependent relations, we might be equally underdeveloped at present due to our own internal obstacles? It is hardly a coincidence that both Spain and Portugal, the colonizers of Latin America, figure among the most underdeveloped countries of Europe. All of this suggests that the internal structures common to Latin American and Iberian countries are the fundamental obstacles to overcoming underdevelopment for us as much as for them.

3. Gutiérrez would say that if underdevelopment in Latin America is not due to dependency, then it is due to capitalism. However, others believe to have found the fundamental reason for present inequality and insufficient development not in the existence of a market economy with private property, but in the initial extreme concentration of economic and political power (since Colonial times) in the hands of a few, and the consequent limitation of opportunities. The United States, where property, power, and opportunities were distributed much more equally from the beginning, was able to overcome its initial dependency as well as underdevelopment. But even in the United States we find notable contrasts. For example, the south of the United States, where power and wealth were more concentrated, only entered into a period of vigorous development during this century, while development was rapid in the center and the west, agricultural regions as well, but characterized by family farms and not large plantations. Moreover, within Latin America it is, in general, those countries in which economic and political power were initially less concentrated—that is to say, the countries of the Southern Cone —where we find a higher level of development. Might it not be, then, that the fault is not to be found in the existence of private property as an institution, but rather in its concentration from the beginning? If this were so, the solution would be in a wide distribution of property, power, and opportunities more than in the suppression of private property and its concentration in the hands of the State.

"Theology of Liberation" and the Social Doctrine of the Church

Although it is not his main concern, Gutiérrez's argument also touches upon various aspects of the social doctrine of the Church. Among others, I would like to emphasize the following:

1. He criticizes the social doctrine's tendency to advocate social harmony as if it were the only way to universalize Christian brotherhood. He considers this a blinder which impedes us from seeing the many conflicting relationships that characterize humanity, most par-

ticularly "the" class struggle, which divides "humanity into oppressors and oppressed, into the owners of the means of production and those deprived of the fruit of their labor, into antagonistic social classes." Any pan-class social doctrine is, under these circumstances, misconceived, if not specious, in that it reinforces the class system.

In my opinion, Gutiérrez is correct in pointing out that acknowledging the existence of a class struggle and trying to abolish its causes is really working towards the construction of the universal brotherhood of man. He is also correct in insisting that the Church's social doctrine has put too much emphasis on the possibility of cooperative relations, more than what is really possible here and now, and not enough emphasis on conflictive relations. Nevertheless, the latter is understandable since the traditional social doctrine does not see the cause of class struggle in the simple existence of private property but rather in the unequal distribution of this property.

On the other hand, it is ideological and ahistorical on his part simply to assert that social relations under capitalism are fundamentally conflictive. For this is to overlook the most significant economic fact of modern times, namely that wealth can be created. In static economies, as were, for all practical purposes, all economies prior to the Industrial Revolution, the economic improvement of some was necessarily obtained at the cost of others.[2] But modern economies are characterized precisely by being dynamic rather than stationary. In a growing economy, everyone stands to gain because more wealth is produced per inhabitant.[3] Hence, the central economic problem since the Industrial Revolution has ceased to be how to achieve and maintain a relatively stable level of production, but how to produce and create more. In such circumstances, the problem of distribution no longer is the paramount preoccupation, as it was in a static, pre–Industrial Revolution economy. In short, there are both conflictive relations as well as relations of mutual advantage or of cooperation, the latter growing in importance precisely since the Industrial Revolution. To be sure, it would be naïve to suppose that

[2] It is not strange, then, that the central concern of static economies, like the medieval one, has been the fixing of just prices and salaries. Moreover, in a static economy, all interest evidently need constitute usury, for capital only reproduces wealth, it does not produce more. Any interest rate means taking advantage of the necessity of the other. In a growing economy, on the other hand, lending capital without interest means sacrificing the additional gains this capital generates. Hence, moral judgments concerning the application of interest changed when the move was made from a static economy to a growing economy.

[3] For example, when goods are exchanged, each of the participants in the transaction considers that his position after the exchange is better than his position prior to it. That is to say, both parties benefit from the exchange.

all social relations are cooperative and deny the existence of conflictive relations. Yet, it would be equally erroneous to found a social analysis on the assumption that all social relations are essentially conflictive, as Gutiérrez seems tempted to do.

2. If it is quite unscientific to deny the existence of social classes, it is a gross simplification to affirm that these are rooted principally or exclusively on property, as Gutiérrez would seem to argue. Social classes are constituted around the different forms of power in a given society. The relative scarcity of that form of power (for example, land, water, transport, capital, technology, knowledge) determines the relative importance of the power-holder, or class. It does not suffice to have property in order to dominate; domination requires the possession of the critical form of power in each historical moment. Moreover, it is not even necessary to possess property to maintain control of basic decisions. Hence, at different times in history the military caste, the clergy, the landlords, the merchants, the industrialists, the bankers, the politicians, the bureaucrats or the technocrats have been preeminent. There is not, then, one single or definite class struggle but many class struggles, although different struggles may come to the fore in each historical moment.

Class struggles will continue as long as there are social classes; and these will go on existing as long as power is unequally held within a society. Concentrate property or whatever other form of power, and classes will be formed and differentiated, and class struggle will ensue; distribute property or any other form of power widely, and social divisions will be minimized. The nationalization of private property will minimize social divisions (it leads to "non-antagonistic" conflicts in Marxist terms) if, as a consequence, the power to make economic decisions becomes truly widespread and participatory. But nationalization will deepen social conflicts (it leads to growing "antagonistic" conflicts) if the participation of the people in these decisions is merely a formality and the real decision-making power is concentrated in the hands of a bureaucratic structure of a partisan nature. In short, it would be hypocritical to deny the existence of class struggles; but it is naïve to believe that such struggles will disappear with the abolition of private property.

3. And the means? It is true—the exaggerated tendency of Catholic theology to interpret social relations as if they were the same as interpersonal relations makes it difficult for the Christian to reconcile social struggle and its instruments of force and coercion with an ethic of love. The solution to this problem lies in the fact that in a social struggle what is important is not to convince your adversary (as is the case of interpersonal relations) but to change his

behavior. Inasmuch as a person's social behavior is to a large extent a product of existing social structures and his position in those structures, and not a product of his own impartial thought, behavior is changed through a change in structures. And structures are changed as much or more by pressure than by reason.

All the same, social liberation cannot be achieved in its *full* dimension through the use of brute power and force. In general, the more advanced or complex the social structure, the more important it is that those affected participate not only in the functioning of the new structure but also in its creation. In effect, we must distinguish between those structural changes that, in themselves, liberate from exploitation and injustice, regardless of whether or not the affected bring about the change (as in the case of slavery), and those structural changes that create conditions for development (such as those found in more advanced social structures—unions, political parties, workers' management) but where the degree of liberation that they represent is in direct proportion to the participation the masses have in effecting them. Hence, a smaller but real structural-institutional development is preferable to a larger structural-formal development but where the participation of the affected is inferior.

To depose the traditional holders of power is revolutionary. But the revolution will not be liberating until such power has been passed institutionally and in fact to the people. The revolution will not be liberating so long as power remains in the hands of a new elite, no matter how avant-garde that elite be.

"Theology of Liberation" and the Church

"If this theological reflection . . . , does not lead the Church in Latin America to take a definitive stand, and without reservations, on the side of the oppressed classes and dominated peoples," concludes Gutiérrez, "it will have served little purpose." So we come full circle.

What action does Father Gutiérrez ask of the Church? To denounce prophetically an inhuman situation. Not only to denounce this evil, but also its causes. Not only denounce in word, but also in acts and deeds.

Yet Gutiérrez simplifies Christian social thinking to a large extent if he believes that he has stated something unequivocal in asking the Church to take a clear position in favor of the oppressed classes and dominated peoples. For, as I have argued above, oppression and domination are not peculiar to the system of private property.

Nevertheless, he is right to emphasize the need of immersing the gospel message in the concrete, in the here and now, if the sense of the transcendent is to be revitalized. It is not a question, of course, of overlooking the transcendental, but of discovering it in the main struggle of our era, the struggle for development. For the transcendental sense when unaccompanied by reference to the concrete tends to result in abstract love, that is to say, in the idolatry of ideas (or ideologization), and not in real love, either of God or of men.

This book also shows the necessity for the Christian message to be expressed in terms of all existing scientific visions. For, although science is by nature reformable, and the Christian message in its essence is not, the message will only be understood if it is first immersed in the prevailing thought of the era. To be immersed is not to be made subordinate; on the contrary, the Christian message will point to those signs of the presence of the transcendental which give life its full meaning, and which are always in danger of succumbing in scientific visions because of the latter's strictly immanent character. This is what Gutiérrez intended to do in this book, integrating his Christianity with the then predominant social thought in Latin America. If I have criticized his work, it is not because of his attempt to link scientific and theological thought, but rather—in my opinion —because of serious deficiencies in the social scientific thought on which he has based his work. But, even if his scientific base is seriously mistaken, his *Theology of Liberation* is an extremely important work, because it shows the ability to assimilate to theological thought new categories of analysis taken from the social sciences, and permits the Christian message to address the real problems of today, and in the way that these problems are lived and felt by Latin Americans.

4

Dependency and Development: An Attempt to Clarify the Issues

Joseph Ramos

Situating the Problem

1. *There can be no doubt as to the existence of dependent economic relations between the center and the periphery, between the United States and Latin America.* More than interdependence between equals, these relations are asymmetrical. A recession or inflation in the United States extends immediately to Latin America, causing recession or inflation in that region. The reverse, on the other hand, does not occur. This is certainly understandable given the relative power of each region: U.S. output is six times that of Latin America. For it would indeed be surprising if the greater power of the United States—which has been reflected in military interventions and "destabilizing" policies—was not also seen in the economic relations between North and South.

2. *Nevertheless, the mere existence of dependency does not mean that the development of the center is due to the underdevelopment (or exploitation) of the periphery.*

   a. Only 5 percent of total U.S. investments are made abroad, and only 7 percent of its production is exported (or imported). For this reason the foreign sector is of little importance to the U.S. economy.

   b. Moreover, the majority of U.S. investments and exports go to other developed countries (Canada, Europe, and Japan); only 20 percent of all foreign investments (1 percent of its total investments) go to Latin America.

   c. The average rate of return of U.S. investments in Latin America does not appear particularly high. For example, the available data (of doubtful reliability, I must admit) indicate that the after-tax profits of U.S. industrial investments in Latin America are of the order of 10 percent on capital, a rate of return higher than that of industrial investments in Canada, but below those in Europe, Australia, Asia, and Africa.

3. While it is clear, then, that the development of the United States cannot be due to the dependency of Latin America, nevertheless it is possible that the opposite is true: that the underdevelopment of Latin America is due to its dependency. The main question, then, is: In what measure is dependency the principal obstacle to the development of Latin America? *It is indisputable that foreign dependency exists, but to what extent does dependency limit the development of Latin America?* The main purpose of what follows is to answer this question.

Recent Events of Importance

Concerning Development. The most important event in recent decades in Latin America has been the economic take-off experienced by the majority of nations on the continent and their entrance into a phase of vigorous and sustained economic growth.

1. Latin America has been growing at a stable pace of 5.2 percent annually for the past thirty years; that is, its per capita income has grown 2.5 percent annually for thirty years (which does not mean that it probably should not or could not grow even faster).

2. Moreover, growth has sped up steadily: between 1945 and 1960 it was 4.9 percent a year; between 1960 and 1970 it was 5.5 percent; and so far in this decade it has been 5.7 percent (despite the post–petrol-crisis world recession).

3. Agriculture, traditionally the most backward sector, has contributed to this development. Not only did agriculture and livestock production grow at a greater rate than the population in the last thirty years (3.5 percent versus 2.7 percent annually), but agricultural productivity has been rising at a rate of 2 percent a year in the same period.

4. Although this development has not benefited all social groups proportionately—which undoubtedly makes distribution the principal challenge for the coming decade (and not development itself)—these groups have experienced important absolute improvements (even though not relative improvements). Aside from improvements in their real monetary income, what most stands out are two social improvements: (i) life expectancy has been extended in the past three decades from less than fifty years to more than sixty-two years; and (ii) education has been tremendously extended. Ninety percent of the school-age population attends primary school today, in contrast with 55 percent thirty years ago; 35 percent of those between the ages of

fourteen and nineteen attend high school today, versus 10 percent thirty years ago; and almost 9 percent of those aged twenty to twenty-four attend university today, versus 2 percent thirty years ago. This implies that, despite existing dependence, Latin America has been able to take off economically and enter into a stage of strong development. The central problem now is no longer development, but the problem of distribution—to increase the participation of these groups that have been left behind in the process of development.

Concerning Dependence. *Recent events in foreign economic relations in Latin America.* The world recession, a consequence of the oil crisis, *lowered* the production of the industrialized countries 2 percent, while in Latin America it only *decelerated growth* to 2.7 percent in 1975; and by 1976, its annual economic growth had climbed back to about 5 percent. Never before had the region shown such vigor and capacity for self-sustained growth. Indeed, it used to be said in the past that when it sprinkled in Europe, umbrellas had to be opened in Latin America. Aside from this outstanding fact:

1. Basic exports were nationalized or larger national control was exercised over them. This was the case, for example, in Chile, with its copper; in Peru, with its petroleum and sugar; in Panama, with the Canal; in Venezuela, with its petroleum.

2. In spite of the prevalent pessimism concerning export possibilities at the time of the Bishops' Conference in Medellin, 1968, we now are witnessing the spectacular rise of nontraditional exports, including industrial exports, in most countries which have attempted a policy of export promotion (Argentina, Brazil, Chile, and Colombia, among others). We are leaving behind, then, the era of import substitution and moving on to one of export promotion.

3. Contrary to popular belief, the fact is that the terms of trade have not deteriorated since the end of the 1950s. If a trend exists at all, it is of an improvement in the terms of trade ever since the early 1960s.

4. Foreign debt has risen rapidly since the oil crisis, from US$40 billion to US$80 billion, in just three years. (This debt, even if it is a potential problem, explains in part how Latin America has been able to maintain its growth during a world recession.)

These events, possibly excluding the last, suggest a reduction of foreign dependence and more strength and autonomy in the Latin American economies.

Dependence and world economic events. Possibly the most decisive economic event for the region is, however, foreign to the region. *The analysis of dependence must be made pre- and post-OPEC, before and after the quadruplication of oil prices (1973).*

1. This shows that *the center is vulnerable* to the *joint* action of the periphery. Even in something as vital for its economies as oil, the center can react moderately and calmly, and accept an important economic loss when it encounters an organized periphery.

2. There has been a notable change in attitude concerning raw materials since the oil crisis. The pessimism about the supposed negative tendencies in the periphery's terms of trade and raw material has disappeared. Today natural resources, *especially nonrenewable natural resources,* are thought to have a great potential value. (Of course, it could be a short-lived hope, but at least it has been responsible for larger investments to find new deposits, and it has led to an improvement in their price.)

3. As a result of the oil crisis, for the first time since the depression of the 1930s, an international capital market has been created, to which the nations of the periphery have access. This market was created with the "tax" levied on oil-importing countries, which became the surplus of the OPEC countries. In the past, these funds remained within the center. Now they are available to the periphery, which explains why foreign lending to Latin America rose from US $3 billion in 1970 to US $15 billion in 1975; and most of these funds came from private international banking.

These events definitely suggest a larger degree of maneuvering and self-sustained development for the periphery.

Implications

The fundamental economic problem of Latin America is no longer development nor dependence, but the problem of distribution. Despite its dependence, Latin America has entered a stage of strong, self-sustained growth. What remains to be solved, however, is the extreme poverty of a significant part of its population. Nevertheless, the means to solve this problem are now within our hands, for it can be solved with the new resources economic development has made available. Whether we decide to use these resources or not is a matter of political will. With political determination we could eliminate extreme poverty, even within the limitations imposed by our foreign dependence, since it is a matter of redistributing less than 10 percent of our national product. Obviously improved foreign economic relations could help in this task, but that is not the central obstacle to eliminating extreme poverty. Its remedy is now in our hands.

Some Economic Problems of the
External Sector in the Future

Though in my opinion dependence is the central obstacle neither to development nor to a better distribution of income, nevertheless the periphery can improve the benefits obtained from its external economic relations.

The periphery can profit from its relations with the center in four ways: (1) by importing capital, which is the most scarce factor, in order to create more jobs with higher levels of productivity; (2) by exporting its abundant labor force, especially the unskilled, through migration; (3) through the export of products that require important inputs of labor; and finally (4) by taking advantage of the technological developments of the center, without incurring the costs of such research and development. In general, the center has restricted each of these flows, since it is easy for the center to block them, notwithstanding their importance for the periphery. Lifting each of these barriers should be the main objective of our foreign economic policy; impeding further restrictions should be our minimum objective.

A word about each of these four points.

1. As I see it, the central problem with the flow of foreign capital is not so much the profits obtained at the expense of the periphery, as how small the flow of capital has been (at least until the oil crisis). Indeed, it is estimated that the United States would have to export ten times more capital than it does presently to reach the levels of England's capital exports during the nineteenth century (given its level of development).

It is undoubtedly true that at times foreign investors have reaped high profits. Exploitation has often been the result of our own mistaken policies, however, and not of foreign capital's greediness (for example, protective tariffs that virtually guarantee high profits by eliminating foreign competition). At other times, the apparently undue profits of foreign investors are merely a reflection of confused ideas. Among the most common, for example, is the argument that foreign investment is undesirable because it takes more, in amortizations and profits, out of the host country than it brings in, as if this were not a necessary condition for every investment (at least as long as it is not a bad investment, meaning one that has failed to create new wealth). For even the "softest" loan possible—one that pays no interest the first ten years and only 3 percent annual interest thereafter—eventually takes out more in amortization and interest than the original investment brought in. Obviously, the correct criterion cannot be whether more wealth is taken out of the country than is put in, but first whether more wealth is taken out than is created and second, what proportion of this new wealth remains.

In my opinion, what is most to be feared in this regard is whether, after the recovery from the center's recession, the capital which is now available for loans to the periphery will return to the center or not. The current ready flow of capital to the periphery could be interrupted through market inertia or through direct limitations imposed by the center on the free flow of capital toward the periphery.

2. Insofar as the migration to the center of the periphery's abundant and unskilled labor force is concerned, not only does the center impose stringent barriers to migration, but its right to do so and unilaterally to limit access to job opportunities there is not even morally questioned. Nevertheless, this "protectionism" is just as damaging to the periphery, if not more so, as the center's tariffs on the periphery's exports. It is important to recall in this regard that it was in large part due to the possibility of exporting its abundant, unskilled labor force that Europe was able to attain the level of development it did in the nineteenth century.

3. Years ago it seemed a remote possibility that the periphery would be able to export industrial products to the center at competitive prices and quality. Today the examples of Argentina, Brazil, Colombia, Chile, Uruguay, Mexico, Korea, and Taiwan, among others, show this is clearly possible. What is doubtful, however, is whether the center will tolerate it; or if, on the contrary, it will give way to the protectionist pressure of its affected companies (almost exclusively domestic companies and not multinationals, incidentally, for the multinationals are by nature much more linked to the export sectors of the center as well as the periphery and, therefore, have the most to lose, at both ends, from a protectionist policy in the center).

4. Until very recently, the normal way to import technology was through licensing or the direct investment of a multinational company. The problem with this, of course, is that the multinationals will prefer maximizing their global rather than their national profits, and that, because of their global character, they are less susceptible to controls imposed by the host country. This is not, in itself, a sufficient reason to reject such investments, but by tying the importation of technology to the entrance of capital, the multinationals do limit the host country's freedom of action. The ideal would be to be able to buy *separately*, and according to the specific needs of the country and sector, the technology, or marketing channels, or management skills, or financial capacity of the multinationals, or any com-

bination of these, without necessarily having to buy the whole package offered by the multinational companies. This should be the basic objective of any negotiations with them. The existence of an international capital market (like the one recently created), with access to it by all countries of the periphery, would facilitate these negotiations enormously. For it has often been the absence of alternative financing which has forced nations to resort to the multinationals (or, in their absence, to autonomous state companies, which, along with the multinational companies, have undergone enormous growth in the last few years, since they are the only ones capable of financing major projects). In this sense, the existence of an international capital market will strengthen the negotiating power of periphery countries by permitting them to purchase separately the different attributes of the multinational companies, thus allowing the host country to choose only what it most needs.

In synthesis, the strategy of the periphery must tend to increase and to separate the flows of capital, labor, trade, and technology between the center and the periphery, and to reduce all legal barriers to this effect. In any case, regardless of what is achieved in this respect, we must remember that stronger growth and a better distribution of income will *not* depend so much on foreign capital, or foreign technology, or foreign entrepreneurs, or foreign demand, as on our own internal efforts in that direction. *Economic development and the elimination of poverty do not depend so much on what others do for us, but on what we do for ourselves. Despite our dependency, we have a sufficient degree of freedom to eliminate these problems with policies within our reach;* none of which excludes, I repeat, parallel efforts to enlarge our freedom vis-à-vis the exterior.

5

On the Prospects of Social Market Democracy—or Democratic Capitalism—in Latin America

Joseph Ramos

The Bias against Democratic Capitalism

A striking feature of Latin America to a Western observer is the intellectuals' low regard for capitalism and their predilection for some kind of socialism (though most frequently for a not yet historically existing brand of socialism). There would seem to be ethical, rational, and empirical objections to capitalism in Latin America:

1. The ethical objection is that it is hard to be excited by a system based on harnessing the lesser elements in man if there is an alternative that appeals to the best in him (from each according to his ability, to each according to his need). Capitalism and the market may be more realistic for man as he is here and now, but if they are, they would seem to be so at the expense of, or in disregard of, his better, potential self.

2. The rational objection is that a planned economy seems far more intelligible than a market economy, which relies on the apparent chaos of supply and demand for allocating resources. This belief is especially widespread among people with little management experience (most intellectuals), who are thus unaware both of the complexity of allocative decisions in the face of myriad considerations and of the market's remarkable efficiency in conserving preciously scarce decision-making capacity for only major decisions.

3. But certainly the most powerful objection is an empirical one. Capitalism has been tried for some 450 years in Latin America and has been found wanting. Had it been effective, Latin America would have a similar level of development as the United States and Europe.

So reads the indictment against capitalism. As for democracy, it is, of course, prized in the abstract, but it is regarded as having been most frequently experienced in its forms, not in its substance.

Democracy is often thought of as formal, not having gone much beyond the written constitution (thus *one* of the explanations why bourgeois democracy—the term if not the reality—is looked upon with such disdain).

Simply, and undoubtedly too simply put, most intellectuals have tended to view Latin America as having had formal democracy but without freedom and participation, and as having experienced a capitalism without growth, characterized by stagnation and concentration. The military, the Church, and the landowners were the real wielders of power, while the rest of society stagnated. Such a simple, almost caricatured view of society was probably not far from the truth for most countries through World War II.

The Onset of Modern Reformism

This assessment gave rise to two major schools of thought. The first, the Marxist school, ascribed the source of the malaise to the system, the capitalist system. This assessment took time to take hold, because dispossessed groups were insufficiently organized, because less radical approaches had not yet been tried, and because, as was well known (at least to intellectuals), socialism would come only after capitalism had matured. Yet clearly, capitalist modes of production were far from advanced in Latin America. The second school of thought, reformism (or populism, as it would later be called as it fell into disrepute), had two principal objectives: to widen suffrage and participation, expanding education, and thus making the system democratic in fact; and to have the state intervene actively in the economy. The problem was considered to be that Latin America had had capitalism without capitalists, so it was up to the state to exercise the entrepreneurial function which the satisfied wealthy and privileged were unwilling to do (because they lacked the drive of the Protestant work ethic).

This explains, I might add, why the state in Latin America is today so large, even in avowedly capitalist economies such as Brazil.

Radicalism, Dependency Theory, and Liberation Theology

For various reasons too complex to go into here, it generally proved easier to expand political franchise and to increase the demands on the state than to expand output and satisfy these demands (an imbalance often called populism). As a result, these systems underwent crisis and positions polarized, resulting for the most part in military governments with a technocratic bent (the first of this new type occurring in Brazil in 1964). The apparent failure of reformist policies—and certainly of reformist parties—led to a rethinking about alternatives. Radicals concluded that the time for socialism had come. Reform was impossible because capitalism in Latin America was not of the same type as capitalism in Western Europe and the United States. This was a *dependent* capitalism, not an authentic capitalism, lacking in entrepreneurship, identifying with foreign (multinational) not national interests, imitative of the consumption patterns of capitalists elsewhere, but incapable of or uninterested in innovation and self-sustained growth. Latin America, it was argued, had experienced a backwash form of capitalist development, not an economically progressive form. Its dependent capitalism was beyond reform, so the continent would need to move directly to the socialist stage of development. This was the essence of the dependency theory of development. It was a hybrid of Marx and Rostow. Latin America's capitalism had proven itself incapable of self-sustained growth, but was instead dependent on the pull of the center. From there it was a small step to argue that its dependency resulted from the imperial exploitation of the capitalist center (and not from its deficient internal social structures).

It is ironic that this negative assessment of Latin America's potential to enter a period of self-sustained growth (and in this sense to overcome its real dependency) took place precisely in the 1960s, a decade unsurpassed in growth in Latin America (and a decade preceded by fifteen years of solid and steady growth ever since World War II). But this growth was not seen; or where it was seen, it was contrasted with hopes and expectations. The society became increasingly polarized with, on the one side, those (the philo-Marxist left) who felt that the system (capitalism) had to be replaced by socialism, and on the other side those of the new right (bureaucratic, technocratic authoritarianism) who argued (and acted via coups) that political participation at early stages of economic development was premature, simply leading to demagogic promises and abuses. To make capitalism work, democracy would need to wait.

Liberation theology was first formulated and developed in Latin America in this context in the late 1960s. In a nutshell, it argues:

1. That there is not only personal sin, but social sin as well. Morality is not just a question of being honest and decent in our personal relations; we must do our utmost to ensure that those relations take place within a just framework. Christian love is not just, for example, a question of treating one's slaves decently. The point is that one must not engage in any relationship (such as slavery) that is essentially unjust and one-sided. The Church was criticized for hav-

ing emphasized private morality almost exclusively, at the expense of social or structural morality.

2. That the central social problem of Latin America today is its underdevelopment, the poverty, both material and social, to which the majority of its population is subject. Yet poverty is no longer inevitable. We possess the means to resolve it. Hence, all Christians are morally obliged to work toward that end. This means that the path to salvation in Latin America requires working for the development (liberation) of the continent's teeming masses. To seek salvation without participating in this great task is pietistic individualism of the worst form, a caricature of Christ's saving message.

These first two theological points are both orthodox and convincing. The next step joins these theological premises to the earlier sociological assessment, giving rise to liberation theology in its most common form.

3. Since development requires overcoming dependency and capitalism, the path of liberation is a call for all Christians to work for socialism in Latin America.

Two tendencies thus marked Latin America in the late 1960s: (1) The increased radicalization of most intellectual currents in the region, culminating in the late 1960s in dependency theory and liberation theology, both of them neo-Marxist in their concerns and outlook. (2) The decline of reformist parties in the face of an increased political polarization, which gave rise to military coups, generally of an authoritarian, technocratic, and capitalistic bent.

Opposed to each other as are these two polar views, both share a disdain for pluralist reform, to which they attribute the worst abuses. The neo-Marxist (not to mention the Marxist) left sees in pluralist democracy an obstacle to radical redistribution (for the left is willing to redistribute wealth and power at any cost); and it regards democratic forms as a façade and rationalization of the status quo. The authoritarian right sees pluralist democracy as luxury, and something to be concerned about only after economic development has taken place (for it is willing to achieve economic growth at any cost).

The Return of Reform

Happily, today there seems to be a swing back to center positions—reform within pluralist structures—and away from polarization (at least for most of the continent outside of Central America). This is in part the result of two important experiences: (1) the existence of authoritarian regimes has shown many (even those on the left) that so-called bourgeois rights and democratic prerogatives were not specious. Though not ideal, in practice they were qualitatively distinct and superior, concerning individual and social rights, to the situation that exists under authoritarian regimes (of both left and right); (2) the realization that in the period since World War II—when reformism flourished—Latin America experienced a rate of economic *and* social progress unsurpassed in its previous 450 years, less than what one might have hoped, but far more than its historic rates and those of Western Europe and the United States. Moreover, that growth has been self-sustained; it is no longer dependent exclusively on Europe and the United States. Whereas output actually declined in Europe and in the United States during the post-1973 recession, growth in Latin America merely decelerated, but output continued to expand.

It is ironic but true that reformism waned as reformist policies succeeded. Not all reformist policies were successful, to be sure, but especially successful were those that universalized education (primary), professionalized private and public management, and reformed land tenure in the countryside. These, in effect, attacked the central malady of Latin America since its colonization—the monopoly of economic, political, and social power in the hands of a small elite— and worked to distribute power and wealth and access to these among a greater part of the population. Thus, by harnessing the efforts of millions of previously dispossessed trying to improve their own lot, reformist policies are transforming Latin America's elite, monopolistic, and aristocratic capitalism into more of the substance and less of the parody of democratic capitalism it used to be. In so doing, they are finally laying the broad foundations necessary for the possible emergence of social market democracies in the continent.

6

Latin America: The End of Democratic Reformism?

Joseph Ramos

The Issue

Undoubtedly the single most powerful argument against democratic or open political systems in Latin America is that they are too weak, too ineffective, too slow, too corrupt, too inefficient to achieve the structural transformations indispensable for economic development. This is not just a criticism from the left but from the right as well. For the left, reform is but a Band-Aid and democracy a mere façade. For the right, reform is nothing but cheap populism, and democracy a form of pork barrel demagoguery, which simply postpones the inevitable day of reckoning.

These judgments do not simply reflect a theoretical bias. Both feed on the generally recognized failure of majestic programs such as the Alliance for Progress to achieve their social and economic goals, and on the notorious and tragic demise of reformist political movements (for example, Eduardo Frei's Christian Democrats in Chile, Victor Raul Haya de la Torre's American Popular Revolutionary Alliance in Peru, Fernando Belaunde Terry's Acción Popular in Peru, and Juan Bosch's Partido Revolucionario Dominicano in the Dominican Republic). From this it is not difficult to conclude that economic development is practically impossible within an open political system.[1] It is then a question of values and of strategic considerations whether one opts for an authoritarian regime of the right or of the left. The rejection of a democratic reformist route to development is common to authoritarian regimes of all types—whether reactionary (Augusto Pinochet Ugarte's Chile), self-seeking (Anastasio Somoza

[1] See Samuel Huntington and Joan Nelson, *No Easy Choice* (Cambridge, Mass.: Harvard University Press, 1976) for a well-reasoned if pessimistic analysis of the problems of achieving economic and political development in the third world.

Debayle's Nicaragua), populist (Velasco Alvarado's Peru), or revolutionary (Fidel Castro's Cuba)—and rationalizes their suppression of social freedoms and basic individual rights.

Ill-posed though I think such a dilemma between political and economic development may be—leading almost inevitably to the conclusion that participation and political development is a luxury for underdeveloped countries, that economic growth must come first—insofar as this dilemma is based on the *economic failures* of reformism, a rereading or really a reading of the economic data (for these have rarely been but skimmed over lightly) on which these judgments rest may prove useful.

The data will show that, contrary to popular belief, reformist policies (not necessarily reformist parties) have been quite successful in achieving *economic growth* in Latin America, though obviously they have shown little success in achieving political development. The tendency of most observers to exaggerate the failures and overlook the successes has meant that the single most important fact in Latin America's recent economic history has gone unsung and unnoticed—namely that Latin America has clearly *taken off* economically, and has entered the stage of self-sustained growth.

The Facts

Since everyone "knows" that the Alliance for Progress was a failure (and in its rhapsodic pretentiousness it was), most readers will probably be surprised to learn that since 1960, gross national product in Latin America has grown at the rate of 5.6 percent a year, well above the goal of 5 percent a year that was considered ambitious in 1960; that, notwithstanding the accelerated population growth of the 1960s, per capita income nevertheless has grown at an average of 2.7 percent a year between 1960 and 1976, not only above the goal set by the Alliance for Progress, but greater than the average growth in the United States in the last one hundred years.

Moreover, such growth has been accelerating. It rose from 5.3 percent a year in 1960–1965, to 5.7 percent a year in 1965–1970, to 6.7 percent a year in 1970–1974 when the world recession set in. But whereas the world recession *lowered* gross national product in the United States and Western Europe by 2 percent (1974), it slowed growth in Latin America, but did not stop it. Output grew 2.7 percent in 1975 in Latin America (when the lowered demand of the industrialized nations affected its exports), but by 1976 it was up to 5 percent. This is a resilience not shown before in Latin America: it used to be said that a drizzle in Europe turned into a hurricane in Latin America.

Nor is this growth simply a phenomenon of the last sixteen years. Strong growth has been under way ever since World War II. Between 1945 and 1960, gross national product in Latin America averaged an annual growth of 4.9 percent. Economic growth in Latin America has thus been proceeding at a rate of 5.2 percent a year now *for more than thirty years*, giving the region a per capita income today of about 1,000 dollars a year. This growth is not limited to only a few countries. On the contrary, except for Haiti, Honduras, Paraguay, Uruguay, and Chile since 1970, all other Latin American countries have grown at least at the rate of 2 percent per capita since 1960.

This growth has not only been strong in manufacturing (6.5 percent a year since World War II), but also in agriculture, where it has averaged 3.5 percent a year in the last thirty years. Moreover, agricultural growth has substantially exceeded population growth (2.7 percent a year), and agricultural output per worker has been increasing at a rate of more than 2 percent a year in the same period. By contrast, since these numbers may not mean much as they stand to the reader, U.S. agricultural output grew at only 2.1 percent a year from the end of the Civil War to the end of World War I, less than population growth for that period, and agricultural output per worker grew at 2.5 percent a year.

Wages and salaries, though apparently growing less on the average than incomes from capital, and thus evidencing a worsened *relative* distribution of income, have nevertheless grown significantly, at some 2 percent a year in real terms. This is still something of an achievement if we consider the strong growth in population and in the labor force in the period after World War II. In the United States, for example, in the fifty years after the Civil War when immigration increased the U.S. population and labor force at rates similar to those of Latin America, wage earnings increased *less* than in the period after World War II in Latin America.[2]

Finally, some of the most spectacular achievements are not registered by economic indicators at all. Life expectancy now averages sixty-two years; infant mortality has been reduced to eight per thousand. How are we to value this extension of life and reduction in illness? Just as important, the last thirty years have seen education finally become widespread; it is no longer the privilege of the elite. Illiteracy has been reduced from just under 50 percent at the end of World War II to less than 25 percent today; it is now largely limited

[2] The United States need hardly be the standard, and less so nineteenth-century America; yet such comparisons are useful in suggesting that this type of situation is more common than most Americans, both North and South, are apt to believe.

to older adults. More than 90 percent of the primary school age population now attends school, more than 35 percent of 14–19 year olds
attend secondary school, and almost 9 percent of 20–24 year olds
attend the university. At the end of World War II these same per-
centages were of the order of no more than 55 percent, 10 percent,
and 2 percent, respectively. This is all the more stunning in that it
took place precisely in a period when the population soared.[3]

Interpretation

Such growth is, of course, relatively new, since World War II. Had it
been going on at these rates since independence, Latin America
would be as economically developed as is the United States today.
The enormous differences in the levels of development of each is, to
be sure, the best evidence of how new such growth is for Latin
America (as a whole). The acceleration in growth is thus not only
strong, continuing, and persistent, but recent. Latin America is beyond the take-off and is well within the stage of self-sustained
growth.

To what is this take-off and sustained postwar growth due?
Certainly not to the largesse of foreign aid or foreign investment,
since net foreign capital accounted for less than 4 percent of annual
investment in the region in this period. Certainly not to especially
favorable terms of trade—which, though fairly steady over the last
thirty years, were low when compared to what they had been in
the nineteenth century. Certainly not to major *visible* structural
transformations, such as land reform (there were few real ones), tax
reform, or the creation of planning offices (largely powerless). I attribute it to Latin America's finally having taken advantage of the
technological, organizational, and management gap existent between
it and the developed world: the advantage of the "late starter," as

[3] The reader may well wonder how it is that such facts—if not the whole picture,
certainly the better part of it—could have been overlooked by most observers.
Apart from those with a vested interest in discrediting achievements, most
observers are apt to feel that the achievements are not good enough, they do
not meet the needs (obviously not), nor possibilities (probably not; more could
be done). Hence, the desire to do better focuses on obstacles and failures rather
than on achievements. Furthermore, most negative readings of recent Latin
American history tend to focus on the period 1955–1960, the only postwar period
when growth did decelerate (to 1.5 percent per capita), when the terms of trade
did worsen, and when population growth did accelerate strongly. Then, too, the
fact that most Latin American social scientists come from the southern cone or
work in the United Nations Economic Commission for Latin America (ECLA),
based in Santiago, made them see the rest of Latin America through the lens of
the poor, and often tragic, experience of the countries of the southern cone. Thus
was the forest lost for the trees.

Thorstein Veblen called it. The opening of mass education and the accelerated professionalization of management and government since World War II have finally turned this technological gap into an advantage.[4] What development could take place fifty years ago in Latin America depended exclusively on a small and contented elite that controlled virtually all capital, education, and access to know-how. What could the 80 percent of the population that was barely literate do for itself? Today, those masses, as well as the elites, are agents in the diffusion of know-how and technology. The masses can help themselves. The technological and human capital revolutions in postwar Latin America are probably the most important explanations of Latin America's postwar take-off. They probably also explain why those last in line to diffuse or introduce new technology—the marginal groups—have received less than their full share of the benefits of this increased productivity.

Significance

It is not the economic interpretation of Latin America's postwar growth that is at issue here, but the *fact* of that growth, and its political implications. I shall not argue, however much I would like it to be true, that open political systems are preferable for economic growth. To be sure, the four longest-lasting democracies[5] in Latin America (Colombia, Costa Rica, Mexico, and Venezuela) have averaged a 6 percent annual rate of growth in gross national product since the end of World War II, well above the region's 5.2 percent average.[5] Yet the two really established democracies, Chile and Uruguay, did rather poorly (Chile grew at 4 percent, Uruguay at 2 percent), and both succumbed to military governments. But certainly the converse is not true. Brazil's strong growth, some 9 percent a year since the military coup, is hardly typical of authoritarian regimes elsewhere. Moreover, Brazil's growth came after fifteen years of solid growth (at 5.5 percent a year) under nonmilitary governments. Military governments in Argentina before the second Perón government averaged no better than 4 percent growth; after three years of military government, gross national product in Chile is still 5 percent less

[4] Twenty years ago most officers of the Agency for International Development (AID) were better prepared than their local counterparts. Today the technical expertise of numerous economists in most planning offices and key ministries exceeds in both formal preparation and experience that of the typical AID economist.

[5] These four democracies are perhaps a far cry from ideal democracies, but in a world of closed authoritarian regimes, one must not knock, but celebrate these countries' willingness to submit regularly to the judgment of the polls.

than the 1973 low of the government of Salvador Allende, and what are we to say of poor Haiti under Papa Doc and Baby Doc Duvalier? Nor has there been any significant difference in economic growth rates between pre- and post-military coups in Panama and Peru. And the longer-standing military governments of Paraguay, El Salvador, Guatemala, and Honduras have done no better than average.

The conclusion that emerges is rather obvious. If Latin America has shown significant and sustained rates of growth for the last thirty years under traditional, paternalistic, populist, reformist, and authoritarian regimes, it is then not the political character of those regimes that explains growth. Rather, it is the set of policies that they have taken in common that explains it. The spreading of education, the raising of savings, the professionalization of management and government explain the rapid introduction and diffusion of modern techniques and technology that account for such growth. And such policies are a good part of what reformism is all about. Reformist policies work. These explain Latin America's take-off. It is not the degree of authoritarianism that explains Latin America's recent successful growth. It is the extent to which fairly simple, reformist policies have been applied. Such is our thesis.

Policy Implications for the United States

Were economic growth to be difficult to achieve, sacrifices—both political (authoritarian regimes) and distributive (to raise investment)—would be understandable, if not fully justified. But if economic growth rates are proving relatively easy to achieve, as postwar Latin American growth has amply demonstrated, then let us sacrifice economic growth for the sake of what has proven almost impossible to achieve: political development and a more equitable distribution of the benefits of such growth. For much as the last thirty years in Latin America have revealed that economic growth is easy to achieve and here to stay, they have also revealed that political development is at a standstill.

There is probably no point in which political and economic development touch each other more closely than on distributive issues. It may be that policies that lead to a more equal distribution of the fruits of growth will slow down economic growth, though this is hotly debated. Many feel that there is still a wide margin for redistribution and for more growth (to the extent that "late starter" growth depends on the introduction and rapid diffusion of new techniques more than on capital accumulation) before such a trade-off, or strong trade-off, would set in. In any case, *there is no doubt that democracy will be all the sounder, not to mention stabler, as property and income are more widely distributed in a society.*

I am of course aware that the pursuit of such a redistributive policy may be so premature or ill-conceived as to stifle economic growth altogether (Uruguay), or so strong and abrupt as to turn the majority against it (Chile), culminating in military governments. Yet for elected governments to overlook distributive considerations is to discredit democratic parties and reformism in the eyes of the poor, to prepare the ground for the authoritarian left, and so to sacrifice political development altogether (Colombia until recently?). For the only real, nonideological justification for the authoritarian left is that it *does* raise the level of living of the 20 percent most destitute members of society, and quickly. Whatever justification there might once have been for ignoring distributive questions, such reasoning is no longer valid now that economic growth has proven easy to come by and here to stay. With the riddle of self-sustained economic growth solved, there is no longer any possible justification for simply relying on the trickle-down effect to pull these groups out of their current state of destitution.

Nor is this an undue burden on society as a whole. We are talking of, say, doubling the income of the 20–25 percent poorest members of the population in the next ten years.[6] Those 50–60 million Latin Americans presently receive only 5 percent of gross national product, or some 17 billion dollars. It is then merely a question of channeling some $50 billion in new investment to them over the next ten years, or $5 billion a year (supposing a capital output ratio of 3 to 1). This amounts to only 7 percent of probable annual investment in Latin America in the coming years, and less than 20 percent of *public* investment. The instruments could be varied: 25 percent of Latin America's agricultural lands could be purchased *at market prices* for some $25 billion, and sold or given outright to poor peasants. Educational and vocational training programs specially designed to meet the needs of the poorest 20–25 percent of the population (and not as now of the better-off urban and industrial workers), to en-

[6] I am aware that such a reformist approach may be considered too slow. Why not redistribute wealth right now, without payment, all at once? Obviously that might be better and more just, were it not that to do so also takes time—many years of organization and preparation of the populace and the poor to support such a program, and of the opposition not to jettison it. Nor are guerrilla methods any faster, for those can go on twenty years without any success, if they ever do succeed. Radical redistributive policies could obviously be more easily effected under military regimes. But for such an opinion to win sway in the military also takes a great deal of time, and generally loses out to opposing views, not to mention that most military regimes have little taste for political development once they have achieved power.

compass one adult member of each of these families full time for one year, including living expenses, could be financed for some $10 billion. Emergency employment schemes for the unemployed (highly labor intensive, minor urban and rural public works projects) could be financed for *all* of Latin America's eight million open unemployed at a cost of $5 billion a year, thus assuring a minimum income for the down-and-out. Obviously, the variety of programs aimed at the lowest 20–25 percent could include community development, credits to small farmers and artisans, agricultural extension to small farmers (currently it is aimed at the large farms).

The point is that these programs would all strengthen the hand of the presently marginal and poorer members of the populations, integrating them educationally, socially, and economically into their societies. In this way political development would be enhanced at minimal, if any, costs to economic growth, making the few existing open and democratic systems stronger and stabler. To be sure, such decisions and policies are primarily up to the political leaders in each country. Yet there is an important role here for the United States, well beyond the enunciation of principles.

Since economic growth in Latin America has proven relatively durable and easy to achieve, whereas political development and distribution have proven difficult, the United States should limit its aid in Latin America to redistributive projects of the type previously outlined, and end stop-gap balance of payments programs or other growth-centered aid programs. If I have previously detailed what is involved in such a program, it is to show that relatively little U.S. aid, with an appropriate leverage from local funds, could *almost single-handedly* resolve the distributive issue in most Latin American countries. Strengthening the situation of marginal groups in authoritarian as well as in democratic regimes would broaden the potential base of democracy and pressure authoritarian regimes to evolve into more open political systems.

Conclusion

The postwar period shows that Latin America has taken off economically, entering the stage of self-sustained growth, but it has regressed politically. Contrary to popular belief, reformist policies have succeeded in achieving strong and self-sustained economic growth in Latin America. But they have failed in achieving political development. For it is an equitable distribution of wealth and income that is the enduring base of democracy, not economic growth.

If the previous analysis has shown that **strong economic growth** is here to stay in Latin America, and that authoritarian regimes are not necessary for such growth, democratic reform movements must now show that they can handle the distributive challenge. If reformist movements can make the marginal and poorer groups of the society participate equitably in the fruits of growth, the viability of democratic reform alternatives of development will be proved, and the justification of authoritarian regimes of the right and of the left will be eliminated.

7

Extreme Poverty in Latin America

Sergio Molina and Sebastian Piñera

One of the most startling features of Latin America's development from a social point of view is its massive poverty. Poverty has always been with us, but what is truly dramatic is that the notable economic growth of these countries in recent years has had little impact on those who live in poverty.

1. Latin America experienced an economic growth without precedent between 1950 and 1975. In fact, during this period, its per capita income grew at an average of 2.6 percent a year despite an annual population growth of 2.8 percent, a figure that surpasses almost all other regions in the world.

2. Estimates made by the UN Economic Commission for Latin America for the decade of 1960–1970 show that the poorest 20 percent of the Latin American population had a per capita income increase of only 2.9 percent during this period, that is, *of two* U.S. dollars (of 1970).

3. Recent studies of critical poverty in Latin America conclude that in 1970 approximately 40 percent of the population, that is, around 115 million persons, received an income below the poverty line which fluctuated around $200 for that year. The destitution line, corresponding to an income equivalent to the cost of a basket of foodstuffs that provides the minimum amount of calories and protein for subsistence, fluctuates around $100. Nineteen percent of the Latin American population, or about 56 million persons, live below this line of destitution.

These findings have made many profoundly skeptical of the customary supposition that economic growth in itself would solve the

This article is a summary and an extract from a study the United Nations Economic Commission for Latin America (known as ECLA in English and CEPAL in Spanish) is preparing on extreme poverty in Latin America.

problems of poverty, unemployment, and underemployment. In other words, the fruits of economic growth have not reached all sectors of the population equally and if a serious effort is not made by governments and by the more affluent sectors, the coming decades will show the same number of destitute and very poor as now.

The definition of poverty we use here corresponds to a concept of absolute poverty. We will now introduce two analytical tools, the destitution line and the poverty line. The destitution line is equivalent to the cost of acquiring a basket of foodstuffs that satisfies minimum nutritional needs of calories and proteins. The poverty line corresponds to twice the above income, so that a person (or family) can spend half his income on purchasing a subsistence basket of foodstuffs and the other half of his income on other basic needs.

The values of this basket have been estimated in accordance with different prices found in each country, as shown in table 1.

Evolution of Poverty

It is important to determine not only the magnitude of poverty in the region but also its evolution before and after 1970. For this reason we will compare the magnitude of poverty in 1970 with that which existed in 1960 and that which will probably still exist in 1990.

It is estimated that around 1960 close to 51 percent of the population of Latin America lived in poverty and around 26 percent in destitution. This means that approximately 112 million people then lived in poverty and close to 56 million people were destitute.[1] There has thus been a reduction in the percentage of people living in both poverty and destitution. The first was reduced from 51 percent in 1960 to 40 percent in 1970 and the second was reduced from 26 percent in 1960 to 19 percent in 1970. Nonetheless, in absolute terms, the number of persons living in poverty and destitution remained practically unaltered between the years 1960 and 1970.

The challenge for all countries is to see if it is possible to overcome the problem of extreme poverty; hence it is important to analyze the so-called *poverty gaps*. These can be defined in many ways. One of the definitions corresponds to the amount of income that would be necessary to transfer to the poor to move them above the different poverty lines. Depending on the objective of the measure, this gap may be expressed as a percentage of disposable personal in-

---

[1] The estimation of the evolution of poverty is based on the working document by the Project of Critical Poverty, "Do the Poor Benefit from Economic Growth?" and from ECLA's estimations concerning income distribution in Latin America in 1960 and 1970.

TABLE 1

PER CAPITA ANNUAL INCOME OF THE POOR AND DESTITUTE IN LATIN AMERICAN COUNTRIES, 1970

(in U.S. dollars)

Country	Destitution Line				Poverty Line			
	National	Urban	Rural	Metropolitan area	National	Urban	Rural	Metropolitan area
Argentina	117	124	93	124	231	249	164	249
Brazil	85	98	74	98	162	197	130	197
Chile	116	125	96	128	225	249	168	256
Colombia	77	85	66	88	147	170	116	176
Costa Rica	82	95	73	98	152	190	128	195
Ecuador	92	106	83	110	173	213	145	220
Honduras	77	92	71	95	142	183	125	190
Mexico	82	89	70	93	157	179	122	185
Peru	78	88	68	91	148	176	119	181
Uruguay	110	117	88	117	214	234	153	234
Venezuela	130	139	108	144	252	277	189	287

NOTE: To calculate the number of persons who are below these poverty lines, we have used the information on distribution of income available in the cited countries. The figures given correspond to countries that represent 84 percent of the total population of Latin America.

SOURCE: Oscar Altimir, *The Dimension of Poverty in Latin America*.

come, of national income, of gross national product, or of government spending. The poverty gap defined as a percentage of the disposable personal income reached an average value of about 6 percent in 1970 for the region. At an aggregrate level, it would be necessary to transfer to the region's poor 6 percent of total disposable personal income, or 12 percent of the disposable personal income of the richest 10 percent of the population,[2] so that poor groups could attain an income that equals or surpasses the poverty line. This poverty gap expressed in a percentage of the national income and of the gross national product would reach an average value of about 5 percent and 4.5 percent respectively. Nevertheless, when this gap is expressed as a percentage of public spending, its average value goes up to about 22 percent.

This dramatic poverty problem is related to the rapid population growth of the region, which is expected to diminish slightly. The present population growth rate of 2.8 percent will fall to 2.4 percent toward the five-year period from 1995 to 2000. This means that in the next twenty-five years the population of Latin America will continue to have the highest growth rate in the world. The working-age population, on the other hand, will grow 3 percent in Latin America during this period, while total employment is expected to increase by only 2.2 percent.[3]

This fact deeply influences the poverty problem and it is estimated that, in 1990, at least 25 percent of the population (some 120 million people) will still be living below the poverty line. The gap between rich and poor in absolute terms is growing progressively larger, this notwithstanding the fact that the gap between rich and poor is already profound.

Factors Determining the Unequal Distribution of Income

1. The large differences in the qualifications of human resources and in the ownership of capital stock (land, physical capital, financial capital), together with deficiencies in the workings of the economic system (at least for the poor) plus the weak role of the state in this

[2] ECLA estimates that the richest 10 percent control 47.8 percent of total disposable personal income.

[3] At the end of the century, open unemployment is expected to affect approximately 9.9 percent of the active Latin American population, or 16.6 million people. Underemployment will affect 35 percent, or 59 million people. Thus 44.9 percent, or 75.6 million people, will then be affected by some form of labor underutilization in Latin America.

field, have determined the unequal distribution of income in Latin America.

2. Estimates of the distribution of income in the region indicate that in the year 1970, the richest 5 percent of the population obtained 30 percent of the income, while the poorest 20 percent only received 2.5 percent. This means that, on the average, the income of the first group is approximately fifty times greater than that of the second.

3. Income differentials per employed person explain little more than half the difference between the per capita income of poor and nonpoor households. The rest is explained essentially by differentials in the rates of participation (the proportion of employed persons in relation to the total number of adults in the household) and of dependency (the number of minors in relation to the total number of persons in the household).

4. Even though there is a close relationship between unemployment and poverty, we must point out that the vast majority of heads of households below the lines of destitution and poverty are employed. Nevertheless, a high percentage of them are underemployed, with a work schedule of less than thirty-nine hours per week, and many express an explicit desire for more work.

The Magnitude of Income Redistribution and Obstacles to It

1. To end poverty, it would be necessary to make constant transfers of about 12 percent of the income of the richest 10 percent of the population, or 6 percent of the total disposable personal income of the nation. These figures, in conjunction with the average income level for most countries in the region, indicate that the poverty problem in these countries is basically one of income distribution, and, to a lesser degree, a problem of the low general level of income.

2. Even though the poverty problem for many Latin American countries appears to have a solution (from the point of view of the resources available), in fact the attempts made by some of them to solve this problem have met with very limited success. Some of the reasons for these failures are found in a reluctance and/or a lack of political capacity to tackle the problem; in a lack of knowledge about how to undertake this task for want of an adequate diagnosis, which makes the selection of ways to eliminate the problem difficult; in the belief that growth will take care of poverty on its own; in putting major priorities on other objectives (stability, foreign trade equilibrium, growth).

The Free Functioning of the Market Will Not Solve the Problem of Unequal Income Distribution

1. Economic growth has not resolved the poverty problem, and the automatic functioning of the market is inadequate to distribute resources in such a way as to satisfy the needs of the poor within a reasonable time frame. Only a factor outside the market mechanism, acting either through or apart from this mechanism, can redirect resources to satisfy the needs of the poor in timely fashion and to change the prevailing style of development. This style is characterized by the emphasis it places on satisfying the growing and diversified needs of the middle and particularly upper income groups.

2. Given the complexity and magnitude of the task of eliminating poverty, it seems inevitable that the state be the leading agent in initiating and promoting different actions and policies necessary to accomplish this end.

Areas of Intervention of the State

The General Approach. (1) Adopt measures that would increase the rates of saving and growth and in this way increase employment and labor incomes. Growth at the same time facilitates the application of redistributive measures. This is related to the level of savings and to the quality of investments. (2) Adopt measures that would adapt the productive structure to available resources. This can be done through exchange, tariff, price, and investment policies. (3) Adopt measures that would affect factor and product markets. In the case of factor markets, it is principally a matter of their integration and the use of correct factor intensities. In the case of product markets, efforts should center on eliminating the concentration of those profits originating in existing oligopolistic or monopolistic practices.

Transfer Payments. These policies are characterized by having as their specific objective the reduction of poverty. In general they are directed to specific target groups. These policies can mean a redistribution of income, of consumption, and of existing assets or of new investments.

Organization and Participation. The success of a policy to eliminate poverty and the permanence of its results are related to the degree of social and political support coming from the group they are meant to favor. This means that a strategy to eliminate poverty must consider the promotion of economic, social, and political organizations and the participation of groups that heretofore have not profited from economic growth.

Demography. An attack on poverty in the full context of development will affect, among other variables, the level of income, the mortality and morbidity rates, and the educational level of the poor. This will influence the demographic behavior of poor households and will probably reduce the number of desired children.

8

Conclusion: The Quest for Liberation

Roger W. Fontaine

The theology of liberation is one of many schools of thought that have contended for dominance in Latin America over the past two centuries. Such schools have typically been of foreign origin. In an age when "dependency" has become the catchword to summarize Latin America's difficulties, the region's intellectual dependency is striking.

Liberalism, positivism, and now socialism have attracted not only schoolmen but political leaders as well. A minority of Latin America's clergy (and even fewer laymen) adhere to the theology of liberation today. It is, however, a remarkable example of the power of ideas in the region. In reading the preceding essays, a Christian layman professionally concerned with such matters must ask three questions. First, how valid is the *theology* of the theology of liberation? Second, how scientific is it? Third, what kind of revolution is it likely to produce?

Whenever I hear references to Christian liberation theology and the arguments usually offered on its behalf, I am reminded of Voltaire's famous words: "This agglomeration which was called and which still calls itself the Holy Roman Empire was neither holy, nor Roman, nor an empire."[1] What is meant by the term "Christian liberation theology"? Is it really Christian? Is it a mechanism for true liberation? Because liberation theology has a certain fashionableness, it is imperative that this ideology be subjected to critical evaluation. It must be examined in its theory, its presuppositions, and its ultimate goals, as well as in its practice, its political programs, and its historical manifestations. Although there is much high-sounding rhetoric in the pronouncements of liberation theologians, as in the recent emphasis

---

[1] *Essai sur les moeurs et l'esprit des nations* (1769).

on "human rights," we must look beneath the rhetoric to discover the true nature of the liberation program. Is it perhaps dedicated not so much to humane values and liberty but to crude anti-Americanism and quasi-Marxist social analysis?

"Latin America," an abstract term of French origin, is inadequate for the diversity of countries it describes. Transplanted priests—those born in Europe or North America, as well as native-born Latins who have studied abroad—perpetuate usage of the term. They speak of Latin America as a single reality; they treat it as a unified entity. Yet what is Latin America? Is it represented by Guatemala or Argentina? Like Chile, Argentina achieved a substantial level of development earlier than many of the other nations. The Southern Cone was, for the most part, ignored by the Spanish colonizers. It escaped colonial, precapitalist exploitation and benefited by virtue of its isolation from the center. Peru and Mexico, which were more desirable to the Spanish, are indelibly marked with the stamp of feudalistic institutions. Given the complexity and diversity of cultures and nations in Latin America, the problem of defining a concrete and descriptive political theology, sensitive to elementary differences, often seems lost behind simplifications.

The strong suit of liberation theology does not appear to be economics, politics, or the philosophy of science. If the "prophetic" refers to the viewpoint that evaluates existing political structures by critical and responsible criteria, then liberation theology does not deal prophetically with the actual political structures of socialism. It seems to concentrate on the *ideals* of socialism. By contrast, it deals prophetically with capitalism only on the critical side, underscoring the evils, unfair practices, and dislocations of that system, with little attempt to describe them fairly. What is needed is a fair, descriptive —perhaps "scientific"—look at the actual practices, past and present, of both capitalism and socialism. This raises the question of the scientific method of liberation theology. Such a stage of inquiry properly precedes prophetic judgment.

One element in the thought of the clerical revolutionaries lies more deeply and firmly in Latin American thought than Marxism. I refer to the synthesis of Christianity and classical paganism exemplified by thinkers like José Enrique Rodó. His thought is best known from, and best expressed in, his book *Ariel*,[2] which William K. Crawford once described as "the pillowbook of a generation of Latin American youth."[3] Rodó was an Uruguayan from the grand bour-

[2] José Enrique Rodó, *Ariel* (New York: Cambridge University Press, 1967).
[3] William K. Crawford, *A Century of Latin American Thought* (Cambridge, Mass.: Harvard University Press, 1945), p. 79.

geoisie who wrote from an aristocratic viewpoint. His own life, attitudes, and thought are quite compatible with those of the clergy, who share a similar background and mingle with commoners only in adult life, their privileges intact.

Rodó was an aristocrat by temperament—an ardent antiegalitarian who believed in the rule of the *aristoi*. He rejected Nietzsche's hatred for the common run of humanity, believing democracy was inevitable. But democracy had to be tempered with the "rule of the best" while the multitude was molded by popular education. Thus there would emerge the few, the best, "to bring to light each human superiority, wherever it exists."[4] Rodó's *Ariel* is a classic expression of an aristocratic democratic theory not uncommon in Latin America.

Rodó's call for a synthesis of Christianity and classical paganism was not, he thought, universally applicable. He felt that Latin America was capable of following such a vision whereas North America was not. The United States, despite its great material achievements, was in his view incapable of the political sophistication required for aristocratic democracy. It was more likely to develop into a meritocracy or plutocracy than a society characterized by the rule of the best. Insofar as Latin Americans share this aristocratic point of view, they are likely to misunderstand the North American experiment with democratic pluralism. They are also likely to be persuaded by the Marxian thesis that a new elite representing the working class and the poor is destined to establish utopian hegemony.

Rodó's theories, then, provide a certain rationale for the clerical revolutionaries. Their theological rationale, however, is drawn from biblical interpretation. Yet some reflection on the Scriptures will show that the biblical basis of the theology of liberation is suspect. Bits and pieces of the Bible are cited. Symbols, metaphors, and analogies are selectively arranged—from the story of the Exodus to the chiliastic appeals found in the Book of Revelation. Although on the surface the approach of this theology is biblical, the organizing principle of selection appears to be ideological.

There is, in fact, strong biblical evidence suggesting that the chief premises on which liberation theology rests are at radical variance with the spirit of Christian experience and revelation. (For secularists this discussion may seem vain and irrelevant; for the Christian, however, whose basic beliefs are shaped by revelation, it is important and uniquely relevant.)

Is political and social revolution the duty of Christians? The Synoptic Gospels and St. Paul's letter to the Romans (Matthew

---

[4] Rodó, *Ariel*, p. 319.

22:17–21; Mark 12:14–17; Luke 20:19–26; Romans 13:1–7) deal with the question. The Gospels recount the incident between Jesus and his enemies among the Pharisees who posed a politically provocative question: Is it lawful to give tribute to Caesar or not? The question was politically tricky because the Romans were unpopular in Judea, a subjugated province, and the Roman tax was still more unpopular. Caesar was an autocratic imperialist if ever there was one—a man and a system ripe for challenge from a liberation theology. And, in fact, a liberation theology was present in the Zealot movement, led by young Jews anxious to rid themselves of the Roman occupation through violence, a movement that ended at Masada. Yet, according to the Gospels, Jesus did not seize the clear opportunity to advocate revolution. Instead, he asked for a coin and asked whose image was on it. Jesus said: "Render therefore unto Caesar the things which are Caesar's; and unto God the things that are God's." This may be an enigmatic command, but it is hardly a call for revolution.

The import of this story is reinforced by St. Paul in his admonition to the Romans:

- Let every soul be subject unto the higher powers. For there is no power but of God: the powers that be are ordained of God.
- Whosoever, therefore, resisteth the power, resisteth the ordinance of God: and they that resist shall receive to themselves judgment.
- For rulers are not a terror to good works, but to the evil. Wilt thou then not be afraid of the power? do that which is good, and thou shalt have praise of the same:
- For he is the minister of God to thee for good. But if thou do that which is evil, be afraid; for he beareth not the sword in vain: for he is the minister of God, a revenger to execute wrath upon him that doeth evil.
- Wherefore ye must needs be subject, not only for wrath but also for conscience sake.
- For this cause pay ye tribute also: for they are God's ministers, attending continually upon this very thing.
- Render therefore to all their dues: tribute to whom tribute is due; custom to whom custom; fear to whom fear; honour to whom honour.

(Romans 13:1–7; King James version)

There is, in these words, a theology of the "two realms," sacred and secular, eternal and temporal, religious and political. These passages from the Gospels and from Romans, taken together, suggest a need for a Christian attitude toward political authority that is simultaneously *critical* and *responsible*. They do not call for blind obedience to an omnicompetent state but for commitment to a constant struggle to establish justice and defend the life of the mind and spirit.

Liberation theology also raises a legitimate question concerning the prophetic nature of the Church. By this is meant the Church's role in rendering judgment on men as individuals and on men in collectivities—that is, on the societies within which values and beliefs are embodied. The role model is the tradition of the Old Testament prophets, especially Isaiah, Jeremiah, Micah, Hosea, and Amos. Each of these prophets voiced a judgment on his society's sins; each predicted disaster if God's people did not radically change their ways. Isaiah, Micah, and Amos specifically demand an account from the rich. "Woe to them [that] covet fields, and take them by violence, and houses, and take them away; so they oppress a man and his house, even a man and his heritage" (Micah 2:1–2). The prophets condemn unlawful pecuniary gain and other forms of injustice.

At this point, questions arise over the precise political role of prophecy. Martin Buber in *The Prophetic Faith* stresses in his interpretation of Jeremiah that it is *God* who judges the sins of his people. Prophecy signifies a divine act in which the prophet serves as a mouthpiece for a revelatory message. Thus, Buber wrote:

> After an eventful century Jeremiah, in his position in face of the shaking of the ancient oriental powers, receives the task of seeing all individual things in one and of interpreting the world hour as God's action in history, judgment and renewal. He is appointed (Jeremiah 1:10) "this day over the nations and the kingdoms, to root out and to pull down, to build and to plant." It is not laid upon him to express the different verdicts of God upon the death and resurrection of the nations, but to show God's sway, the pulling down and building up of the world's architect, the rooting out and the planting of the world's gardener. God lets the prophet note His action, as such, in the chronicles of the spirit. That he is "appointed" "to root out" means that he has to *say* of the rooting out that it is such. He has to *say* what God *does*.[5]

The prophetic role of the Church does not mean that Christians are routinely called to make revolution against an unjust political order. They may or may not respond, according to the situation. It does mean that Christians should be critical of political authority and work

---

[5] Martin Buber, *The Prophetic Faith* (New York: Harper & Row, 1949), pp. 165–66.

to make all power accountable to the popular will. Many Christians are highly skeptical of the revolutionary option, however, and believe that the probable result of a revolutionary overthrow of existing regimes will be greater injustice. In actual experience the chaos and suffering generated in such situations are often followed by new forms of tyranny. Much depends on reasonable hope of improvement—on a practical model for an effective liberation.

The second question that must be raised concerning liberation theology is this: Does it lead to true liberation? Or is it merely the continuation of an older tradition by other means? Marxist revolutionaries historically have established rather traditional-looking dictatorships. Rule by force, rule by an elite, is the usual historical outcome. Alleged revolutions often end by being profoundly counterrevolutionary.

Ralph Lerner has pointed out a revolutionary tradition having a radically different view of man, society, and government. It is the tradition of realist revolution, perhaps the only real revolution; it is embodied in the ideas and actions of eighteenth-century political theorists such as Alexander Hamilton, John Adams, and Thomas Jefferson. Jefferson addressed the question of liberty and the role of religion in Latin America in retarding it. In his last extant letter written to Roger Weightman on June 24, 1826, Jefferson wrote: "May it be to the world, what I believe it will be . . . the signal of arousing men to burst the chains under which monkish ignorance and superstition had persuaded them to bind themselves, and to assume the blessings and security of self-government."[6] The realist revolutionaries stood for limited government, constitutionalism, the rule of law, the balance of political powers, and the democratic process in formulating public policy. Their vision was quite different from that of Marxist "liberationists." Although "monkish ignorance and superstition" may have changed from century to century, the effects are the same. Autocracy continues in the twentieth century in new forms, often under the flag of "liberation." What real promise is there that liberation theology will avoid a new form of autocracy—or a new alliance of church and state under socialist auspices? We are still far from achieving Jefferson's vision, in which "the mass of mankind has not been born with saddles on their backs, nor a favored few booted and spurred, ready to ride them legitimately, by the grace of God."[7]

Finally, is the social analysis of the liberation theologians sci-

---

[6] Adrienne Koch and William Peden, eds., *The Life and Selected Writings of Thomas Jefferson* (New York: Modern Library, 1944), pp. 729–30.
[7] Ibid.

entific? I have already mentioned their tendency to compare the ideals of socialism with the practices of capitalism (selectively emphasized). There is a fundamental misapprehension of causality when intellectuals fail to make the connection between the dogmas of an ideology and its historical practices.

What leads to this error in understanding is the Marxist propensity to render judgment *before* social analysis is undertaken. Capitalism is a priori oppressive; therefore, its results can only be evil. Socialism is clear and pure in its intentions; thus its practices can only improve the conditions of life.

Scientific rigor is an old problem in Latin America. Even when the notion of "science" was dominated by the views of the nineteenth-century positivists, little disciplined scientific analysis was accomplished. Social science in particular has been remarkably polemical and politicized in Latin America. It has often remained epistemologically naive. Until greater precision is applied to understanding political and economic realities, it is impossible to elaborate an ethical critique of the situation. The Marxist social analysis cannot account for the complex power realities of modern states, because it cannot meet the demands for objectivity. It is, however, a useful political device for discrediting the status quo. It provides justification for the most ruthless hegemony of an elite claiming to act on behalf of the people. Marxist oversimplifications corrupt the theological and ethical task of formulating a doctrine of justice and order in a fallen world.

Clerical revolutionaries in Latin America call for peace and solidarity and economic justice by cleverly manipulating biblical and theological themes. But what they promise has not yet appeared anywhere. Instead we see coerced uniformity, stagnant economies, and the distribution of privileges according to ideological criteria. In the name of liberation, some reinvent tyranny.

Editor's Postscript

Michael Novak

Thus we conclude this attempt at furthering "the competition of ideas." There are two major traditions of revolutionary political economy in the world, one liberal and the other Marxist. Often, both traditions compete against a backdrop of traditional, often peasant, societies. Each of these revolutionary traditions has many variants, and there are many subtle combinations of both. Key terms have different meanings in different intellectual traditions—liberalism in Latin American history, for example, means something different from liberalism in North American history. Yet, ironically, many people in the religious communities of North America and South America are better informed today about the ideals of a Marxist political economy than about the ideals of a liberal political economy. Christianity, of course, transcends both forms of political economy.

Some may argue that the future of Christianity is better served by marriage to a modified Marxist political economy, whereas others may argue that it is better served by a modified liberal political economy. These arguments are realized in concrete political struggles of an urgent sort.

In the first case, it is important to see that "Christian Marxists" are eager to define their new variant of Marxism in a way that is neither atheistic nor materialistic. In the second case, "liberal Christians" are eager to define their vision of democratic capitalism in a way that is neither solely individualistic nor materialistic.

In the real world of today, however, complex societies seldom exhibit the pure lines of any one theory inherited from the past, whether Marxist or liberal. Still, conceptual ideals such as "capitalism" and "socialism" continue to operate as magnets below the surface. The ways in which they do so are manifold and should be carefully explored.

One obstacle to such an exploration at present is the general lack of clarity about the moral ideals of democratic capitalism. Although there are many books and studies on the ideals of Marxist socialism, on democratic socialism, and also on social democracy, there are very few, if any, works available on the ideals of democratic capitalism. (Good books written by economists such as von Mises, Hayek, and Friedman tend to concentrate more upon the economic system of democratic capitalism than upon the system as a whole, which includes powerful and indispensable political institutions and moral-cultural institutions.) This lack of theory leaves room for many misconceptions. Thus, the superior general of the Jesuits, Father Pedro Arrupe, in his famous letter on the use of Marxism as a method of analysis, comments negatively about the liberal ideal as he perceives it: "The type of social analysis used in the liberal world today implies an individualistic and materialistic vision of life that is destructive of Christian values and attitudes."[1] There are many who embrace the ideal of democratic capitalism, however, who do not concede that it includes either materialism or a non-Christian form of individualism. In a pluralistic society, there are bound to be some persons who are materialistic and others who are radical individualists. Yet theirs is not the only version of the liberal ideal.

One must distinguish, therefore, between versions of socialism—perhaps even of Marxism—that are compatible with Christianity and those that are not. The same necessity affects versions of democratic capitalism that are compatible with Christianity and those that are not.

We hope that the present text—one in a series of works yet to be accomplished—sheds some light on these conceptual matters and on present-day realities. It is not easy to understand the historical currents of our era. Nor is it easy to think or to live as a Christian (or a Jew or a Muslim). To attempt to do both compounds the difficulty. That difficulty can be diminished a little, we hope, by intelligent inquiry and a fresh competition of ideas.

[1] Pedro Arrupe, S. J., "Marxist Analysis by Christians," *Origins*, vol. 10 (April 16, 1981), p. 693.

Contributors

Roger W. Fontaine, former director of Latin American Studies at the Center for Strategic and International Studies at Georgetown University and a former visiting scholar at the American Enterprise Institute, is senior staff member for Inter-American Affairs of the National Security Council.

Ralph Lerner is a member of the Collegiate Division of the Social Sciences at the University of Chicago.

Sergio Molina has served on the United Nations Economic Commission for Latin America (ECLA) and was formerly minister of finance of Chile under President Eduardo Frei.

Sebastian Pinera has served on the United Nations Economic Commission for Latin America (ECLA), specializing in problems of extreme poverty.

Joseph Ramos is professor of economics at the Latin American Institute on Doctrine and Social Studies (ILADES) in Santiago, Chile. He is a former economist at the United Nations and consultant to the Catholic Bishops of Latin America. He is currently a member of the Regional Employment Team for Latin America and the Caribbean of the UN's International Labor Organization.

Juan Luis Segundo, S.J., was born in 1925 in Montevideo, Uruguay. He was ordained priest in 1955. He studied at the Faculty of Jesuit Theology at Louvain and at the Faculty of Literature at the University of Paris. He holds a licentiate in theology and a doctorate in literature. He is former director of the Center at Montevideo for Social Study and Action, the Centro Pedro Fabro, and the author of the five-volume *Theology for Artisans of a New Humanity* and other works.